GODWIN'S
MORAL PHILOSOPHY

GODWIN'S
MORAL PHILOSOPHY

AN INTERPRETATION OF
WILLIAM GODWIN

By

D. H. MONRO

OXFORD UNIVERSITY PRESS
LONDON : GEOFFREY CUMBERLEGE
1953

Oxford University Press, Amen House, London E.C. 4

GLASGOW NEW YORK TORONTO MELBOURNE WELLINGTON
BOMBAY CALCUTTA MADRAS KARACHI CAPE TOWN IBADAN

Geoffrey Cumberlege, Publisher to the University

PRINTED IN GREAT BRITAIN

ACKNOWLEDGEMENTS

MANY individuals and some institutions have helped me to write this book. I was able to begin it in New Zealand with the aid of a research grant from the University of New Zealand for the purchase of books not accessible there, and to finish it in Oxford through the generosity of the Nuffield Foundation, which awarded me a Fellowship. I am also grateful to the University of Otago for granting me leave of absence and to the Warden and Fellows of Wadham College for hospitality while at Oxford.

In the early stages I had advice from Professor J. A. Passmore, of the University of Otago, and at Oxford encouragement and criticism from Professor H. J. Paton, Professor G. D. H. Cole, Mr. W. Harrison, Mr. J. Plamenatz, Mr. I. Berlin, and Mr. P. Nowell-Smith, all of whom have read this book in manuscript. None of them can, of course, be held responsible for its contents.

The substance of Chapter I was originally published as an article in the *Australasian Journal of Philosophy*, and is reprinted by permission of the Editor.

CONTENTS

INTRODUCTION

THE GODWIN LEGEND

WILLIAM GODWIN has figured less in the histories of philosophy than in the histories of English literature, as an influence (and, it is quite usual to add, an unfortunate influence) on Shelley and Coleridge.

As Shelley's father-in-law, he was bound to receive some notice, since the story of Shelley's marriage makes an interesting chapter in any literary history. There is, moreover, an equally interesting story to be told about Godwin's own marriage with Mary Wollstonecraft. Further human interest can be found in the fact that Godwin, in his penurious old age, was not above sponging on Shelley.

These are the scraps of information that generally come to mind when Godwin's name is mentioned. They suggest an unpleasant character: possibly a charlatan, certainly a crank. This impression is not removed by the knowledge that Godwin had some reputation, in his own day, as a philosopher. Especially if his philosophy is encountered in the writings of his political opponents, such as the skilful satirists who wrote for *The Anti-Jacobin*. The student of literature gathers that Godwin had unorthodox opinions, not only on marriage and on the family, but on property and government. His attitude to all these institutions, it seems, was simple. He disapproved of them and wanted to abolish them.

The literary historian has not much incentive to correct these first impressions. Godwin wrote a staggering number of books, including some novels, one of which was a popular success, and a play or two, which were damned. He was also something of a literary historian himself. But, regarded simply as a writer, he is not important enough to be worth more than a few paragraphs. In these circumstances it is at least possible

B

that a legend has grown up round Godwin that does him less than justice.

Before saying more about this legend, it may be as well to give some details of Godwin's life. As this story has often been told before, it can be set down briefly.

William Godwin was born in 1756. His father and grandfather had both been dissenting ministers, and Godwin himself entered the ministry in 1778. Within five years he had lost his faith, apparently as the result of reading Rousseau, Helvétius, and Baron d'Holbach, and he resigned his living and settled in London to become a writer. With the desperate industry of those who must write before they can eat, he produced thousands of words on almost any subject that caught his interest or the fancy of his publisher: a *Life of Chatham*, two vanished novels (one written in ten days, the other in twenty), articles for the Whig periodicals, the historical section of the *New Annual Register*.

In 1791 Godwin managed to free himself from this hackwork, at least for the time being, by persuading his publisher to finance him while he settled down to a serious treatise on political theory. He spent nearly two years writing it; but the publisher's speculation was a shrewd one. The *Enquiry concerning Political Justice* was an immense success. Indeed, if it had not cost three guineas, the Government of the day would have banned it. With passionate sincerity and a complete absence of compromise, Godwin had set down the radical beliefs that were emerging from the French Revolution and the intellectual ferment that had preceded it. This was the book the intellectual radicals of the day were waiting for; and Godwin became a celebrity. For a few years he was happy and successful in both his work and his private life. *Political Justice* went through three editions, with Godwin conscientiously making corrections and revisions whenever he thought a critic had made a sound point against him; he wrote a novel,

Caleb Williams, which was widely acclaimed as a masterpiece;
he met and married Mary Wollstonecraft, and was idyllically
happy with her.

Success did not last. The French Revolution began to turn
sour in the mouths of the English intellectuals, much as the
Russian Revolution has turned sour in our own day. Godwin's
celebrity became a bad eminence. He was attacked with the
utmost scurrility, sometimes by his former friends. Mary died.
Godwin wrote a memoir of her which provided his opponents
with some useful ammunition: she was not only a notorious
feminist, the author of the *Rights of Women*, but the victim,
before she met Godwin, of an unfortunate love affair with
Gilbert Imlay. Godwin showed a sympathetic understanding
of her conduct, and a quite indecent fondness for her illegitimate child. *The Anti-Jacobin*[1] commented charitably:

> Being her spouse, he tells, with huge delight,
> How oft she cuckolded the silly clown,
> And lent, O lovely piece! herself to half the town.

Godwin married again. His second wife had no unwomanly
notions; Godwin was not happy with her. He wrote more
books, with varying success: a volume of essays, more novels,
plays, a life of Chaucer, a history of the Commonwealth
period. Before long he was back at hackwork, turning out
children's books, which he published himself. As a publisher
he was not successful, even though his friends Charles and
Mary Lamb wrote their *Tales from Shakespeare* for him. He
was constantly short of money: given, as we are so often
reminded, to borrowing from his wealthier friends; given also,
as we are less often informed, to lending to his poorer friends.
In 1836 he died.

As has been indicated, Godwin is one of those writers who
are seldom mentioned without a sneer. There were obvious
reasons for this in his own time. *Political Justice* was

[1] Aug. 1801, p. 518.

immensely popular during the honeymoon period of the French Revolution. Bliss was it in that dawn to be alive; but dawns do not last. In full daylight Godwinism came to look less attractive; and in the popular mind (still more in the pulpit mind and the press mind) he stood for all the worst excesses of Jacobinism. 'Pure defecated Atheism', said Burke, 'the brood of that putrid carcase the French Revolution.'[1] As de Quincey noted, 'most people felt of Mr. Godwin with the same alienation and horror as of a ghoul, or a bloodless vampyre, or the monster created by Frankenstein'.[2] And anyway, he was unsound on marriage.

None of this is really surprising. In any age denunciations of 'the new morality' (still more, the new politics) are likely to be more colourful than accurate. But what is perhaps surprising is that so much of the mud should have stuck, after a century and a half. In 1920 it was still possible to write of Godwin: '. . . with all his writings he has not left one single phrase with which his name can be associated, or one thought worth thinking. . . . He was a cold, hard, self-centred man who did good to none and harm to many. . . . It is his fate to be remembered chiefly as the husband of the first suffragette.'[3] And the judgement of history (or at least of historians) is delivered in the same tone: 'Godwin is one of those philosophical gas-bags who has been so long pricked and deflated that it is extremely difficult to reconstruct him in the dimensions he assumed in the eyes of his contemporaries.'[4]

Yet one would have thought that much that Godwin stood for would be generally accepted today. Of all the insults

[1] Quoted by Ford K. Brown, *Life of William Godwin* (London, 1926), p. 155.

[2] London reminiscences, in *Collected Writings*, ed. D. Masson (London, 1897), iii, 25.

[3] A. E. Newton, *Amenities of Book-collecting* (Lane, 1920), pp. 246 and 248.

[4] D. C. Somervell, *English Thought in the Nineteenth Century*, 6th ed. (Methuen, 1950), p. 32.

heaped upon him in his own time, one of the most frequent
and the most damning is the term 'Democrat'; and this is a
word which, though it has not lost its powers of incantation,
stirs us today with quite different emotions. Godwin was
ridiculed by his contemporaries for suggesting that a field
might one day be ploughed by machinery, and that man might
learn to prolong his span of life, so as to outgrow the childish-
ness that now afflicts even the most mature of us. The first of
these daring flights of fancy has become a commonplace, and
even the second (which, Godwin insisted, he advanced as a mere
speculation) has at least been able to stimulate Bernard Shaw.

But, it may be objected, if Godwin was sometimes right,
he was right, so to speak, by accident; he was constitutionally
incapable of understanding all the deeper springs of human
behaviour, and all the subtler ties of society. For (and this
is the usual legend about him) Godwin rejected emotion in
all its forms in favour of a bloodless abstraction he called
reason. Family ties, loyalty, patriotism, respect for law, religious feeling—all these he blandly declared to be irrational
and tried to sweep away. In the teeth of all the evidence, he
thought that men were 'naturally good', and needed no restraints but their own intellects.

Young men in love were often observed to attribute qualities to their mistresses that they plainly did not have; mothers
frequently expressed a foolish preference for their own babies
as against strange children who were plainly more beautiful,
more talented, better behaved; men and women alike often
showed a curious resentment when told of their faults, though
clearly they could only benefit from knowing about them.
How unreasonable! Clearly a rational animal would not behave
like this, unless corrupted by those who pretended to govern
him, and by the institutions that tyrants, doubtless for their
own selfish ends, had foisted upon him. To achieve the millen-
nium, nothing was needed but the abolition of law, religion,

and the family. Completely passionless, serenely unaware of all the warmth and colour and tragedy and beauty of human life, 'this cold, hard, self-centred man' (or, alternatively, this well-meaning, good-natured, but essentially obtuse man[1]) went on spinning his syllogisms, while Paris burned and England smouldered. Is it any wonder if people turned away in disgust from his dangerous nonsense?

That is the Godwin legend—parodied a little, I admit; but really not very much. It is usual to add that the young Shelley, who is then described as the most passionate, sensitive and perceptive of poets, whose lack of ordinary human callousness made life unendurable to him, was completely enchanted by Godwin's philosophy.

In spite of this inconsistency, the legend is not without its basis in fact. Moreover, Godwin did have his irritating side. It is quite just to call him a windbag, though unjust to imply that he was nothing else. He was not, I think, cold and hard, and he was not a libertine; but he was rather a prig. I am not, however, concerned with Godwin as a man, but with his ideas. And it is at least arguable that Godwin deserves to be taken more seriously as a philosopher than he usually has been taken.[2] Godwin was not a profound or original thinker; he was given to rhetoric, and he often said a good deal more than he meant, as he himself confesses. But he did sum up the impact of the Enlightenment on the Englishmen of his generation, particularly those Englishmen who had a long tradition of Puritan theology behind them. Godwinism was the offspring of French intelligence and the English nonconformist conscience. It was no accident that it took the young intellectuals of the seventeen-nineties by storm. At the very least,

[1] For this variant of the legend see (e.g.) the *Cambridge History of English Literature*.

[2] I hasten to add that some writers on Godwin have treated him sympathetically, notably H. N. Brailsford; and, more recently, F. E. L. Priestley, David Fleisher, and George Woodcock.

it deserves attention as a chapter in the history of ideas: one that is not without its influence even today.

More specifically, the Godwin legend has ignored or distorted many of Godwin's most characteristic ideas. Briefly, it can, I think, be maintained, against the traditional view:

1. That Godwin was not at all blind to the part emotion plays in human behaviour, and that he did not wish to exclude it. In all his novels the main theme is the wretchedness of the man who is cut off from sympathetic communion with his fellows. He believed, moreover, that all of us are cut off, to a greater or less extent, by our own lack of insight.

2. That the 'reason' Godwin extols is not the manipulation of abstractions, but something like Spinoza's *scientia intuitiva*. He believed that we do not really understand a generalization unless we see in detail how it applies to a particular concrete instance. Since no one instance is quite like another, generalizations are only approximately true. Human beings in particular are each of them unique. We will, then, never understand each other so long as we judge each other by the facile conventions imposed on us by society. Reliance on these is the main cause of that lack of insight that leads to the tragedy of loneliness.

3. That, so far from lacking 'the historical approach', and concentrating on an 'abstract' Man who never existed, Godwin stressed the part played by society in moulding men's opinions and behaviour. The generalizations or conventions which hide humanity from us are very much a social product, and even a political product. It is in that sense that 'government corrupts'.

4. That Godwin's doctrine of 'natural goodness' is not a piece of crass optimism, but an expression of his belief that evil and cruelty are caused by lack of insight.

5. That one reason why Godwin has been misunderstood is that he has been regarded as a political reformer, whereas he was primarily a moralist. As a manifesto or a programme, his anarchism is certainly absurd; but not more absurd than

Plato's *Republic* or Rousseau's *Social Contract*. Like Plato
and Rousseau, Godwin is concerned, not with a political
programme, but with an analysis of society and, above all,
of the causes of 'prejudice', or lack of insight. Regarded in
this light, his anarchism, though no doubt inadequate, is not
obviously absurd or lacking in reality.

These are the main contentions of this book. Let me now
sketch the order in which they are set out. Since I wish to
deal with Godwin as a moralist, I have begun with an outline
of his theory of ethics. Chapter 2 discusses, in greater detail,
his views on the relation between reason and feeling in ethics,
a problem which puzzled Godwin and on which he vacillated
considerably. Chapter 3 deals with Godwin's views on the
influence of society on our behaviour and opinions, and his debt
to Montesquieu. This has led on, in the next two chapters,
to Godwin's criticism of Montesquieu and of the main social
and political patterns that Montesquieu described. From
this criticism it has been possible to obtain Godwin's analysis
of the causes of prejudice, and this, together with his tentative
proposals for curing it, forms the subject of Chapter 6. Since
all this has been largely expository, I have added a chapter in
which I have ventured some criticism of Godwin. It should be
pointed out, however, that I have not confined my criticism
to this last chapter; throughout the book my exposition has
been partly critical.

In spite of that, it will be seen that this book is in a way a
defence of Godwin. I hope, however, that is not merely a
piece of special pleading. I hope, too, that I have not given the
impression that I think myself the first man to whom the truth
about Godwin has been revealed. I have learned much from
all my predecessors, even those who have propagated what I
have called the Godwin legend. I do not think, however, that
either Godwin's critics or his few defenders have brought out
the points that I have summarized above.

1

ARCHBISHOP FÉNELON VERSUS
MY MOTHER

I

WHAT almost everybody knows about Godwin is that he
thought that he ought not to save his own mother or sister
from a burning building in preference to someone, like Fénelon, more likely to contribute to the general happiness. (At
least he thought that in his first edition. In the second and
third, he made it 'father or brother' as a sop to popular prejudice.)

> The illustrious archbishop of Cambray was of more worth
> than his valet, and there are few of us that would hesitate to pro-
> nounce if his palace were in flames, and the life of only one of them
> could be preserved, which of the two ought to be preferred. . . .
> Suppose the valet had been my brother, my father or my bene-
> factor. This would not alter the truth of the proposition. . . . What
> magic is there in the pronoun 'my', that should justify us in over-
> turning the decisions of impartial truth?[1]

In Godwin's own lifetime this was apparently what most
people remembered from *Political Justice*. Lamb refers to him
as 'counsel for Archbishop Fénelon versus my own mother,
in the famous fire cause'. But not much has been said about
the passage, in spite of its notoriety, except that it shows:

[1] *Enquiry concerning Political Justice*, 3rd ed., 1798, i. 127. All quota-
tions are from the photographic facsimile, ed. F. E. L. Priestley (Toronto
U.P., 1946). The illustration may have been suggested to Godwin by a
sentence in Hutcheson: 'Thus, if two persons of unequal dignity be in
danger, we are to relieve the more valuable, when we cannot relieve both.'
(*Inquiry*, Sect. 7; Selby-Bigge, *British Moralists*, i. 170.) Apparently
anticipating the scandalous inferences that might be drawn, Hutcheson
adds immediately: 'We ought . . . to be grateful, rather than Beneficent,
when we cannot (in any particular case) evidence both dispositions.'

(*a*) the absurdities to which philosophers are driven through trying to be logical, (*b*) that Godwin was the kind of tight-lipped moralist who is blind to what makes life really valuable. And it is sometimes added that the conclusion was so absurd that even Godwin could not hold it for long; he expressly withdrew it in his later writings.

None of this is fair to Godwin. It is true that he did not remain satisfied with the position he had reached here, but neither did he simply recant. He was grappling with a genuine problem, a kind of Kantian antinomy of Ethics, and he saw that its solution would go to the heart of moral philosophy. Should we trust to affection or to justice, when they seem to conflict? To decide either way seems to offend our moral consciousness. Rousseau touches on the problem when he speaks of pardons. A pardon is a particular act, which is not merely the application of a general rule: it is indeed its nature to be a violation of a general rule. It is therefore, on Rousseau's principles, not within the competency of either the sovereign, who is concerned only with general principles, or the magistrate, who is concerned only with their application to particular cases. It would seem to follow that criminals should never be pardoned. But Rousseau shrinks from this conclusion: 'I feel my heart protesting and restraining my pen; let us leave these questions to the just man who has never offended and would himself stand in no need of pardon.'[1]

It was not Godwin's way to shirk such problems. If the promptings of the heart really conflict with reason, we must decide in favour of reason. And Godwin does indeed condemn the current practice of pardoning. 'What are the sentiments in this respect that are alone worthy of a rational being? Give me that, and that only, which without injustice you cannot refuse. More than justice it would be disgraceful for me to ask, and you to bestow.'[2]

[1] *Social Contract*, bk. ii, ch. 5.   [2] *Political Justice*, ii. 419.

So far we seem to have the tight-lipped moralist once again. But that is not all. Godwin sees clearly enough why men are disposed to pardon. It is because they realize, though confusedly, that the punishment was not, in the first place, really just. It is merely muddle-headed to affirm with one breath that it is right to punish a man, and with the next that it is right to pardon him. We must not say that justice and benevolence are opposed here, and that justice is an inferior principle. If we are to have a consistent moral philosophy, the two must be reconciled; and they can only be reconciled by a truer conception of justice. To punish and to pardon cannot both be right; but Godwin's final conclusion is that it is punishment that is wrong.

Rousseau's dilemma, Godwin suggests, points to a fundamental defect in his whole political theory. Rousseau's basic assumption is that the rule of law must be right. The sovereign people cannot go wrong so long as it confines itself to framing general principles which are to be applied impartially to all individuals. It goes wrong only when it makes exceptions in favour of the individual, when it sacrifices the public interest to the private interest. This is the principle of impartiality which Godwin is applying when he comes to consider 'the famous fire cause'. But, because he is prepared to apply it rigorously, as Rousseau was not, he sees that it is defective. We do not attain to justice by applying general rules, without fear or favour, to particular cases; because general rules never do apply to particular cases.

There is no maxim more clear than this: every case is a rule to itself. No action of any man was ever the same as any other action or had the same degree of utility and injury. It should seem to be the business of justice to distinguish the qualities of men, and not, which has hitherto been the practice, to confound them. . . . The fable of Procrustes presents us with a faint shadow of the perpetual effort of law. In defiance of the great principle of natural philosophy, that there are not so much as two atoms of matter of the same form, through the whole universe, it endeavours to reduce the actions of men, which are composed of a thousand evanescent elements, to one standard.[1]

No man has insisted more strenuously on the appeal to reason than Godwin. But the reason to which he appeals is not the tight-lipped morality that lays down rigid formulas. Still less is it the abstract logic that ignores men in its search for Man. Next to the paragraph about Fénelon, the most quoted passage from Godwin is probably the one in which he objects to our telling unwelcome visitors that we are 'not at home'. But although Godwin insists, almost as strongly as Kant, on the virtue of truth-telling and the necessity of absolute sincerity, he does not regard moral rules of this kind as the final deliverances of Reason. They are only 'resting-places for the mind', and this is probably his view even of the greatest happiness principle itself. Godwin is well aware that the greatest happiness is itself an abstraction: that there is only the happiness of individuals. The reason to which he pins his faith is, in the last analysis, something like Spinoza's *scientia intuitiva*. We progress from abstract generalization to grasping the particular in all its particularity.

In the problem of Fénelon and his valet, and in the problem of pardons, Godwin is grappling with the conflict between justice and love. It might seem that he solves the first in favour of justice, and the second in favour of love. But there is no real inconsistency here. No really satisfactory solution of the fire problem is possible, because the situation is inherently evil. The terms of the supposition are that we cannot save both. When we are faced with such hard choices, we are not indeed entitled to consider our own pleasure, if this results in the greater pain of other people. This is the only ground on which Fénelon should be saved: that his continued exis-

[1] *P.J.*, bk. 7, ch. 8, vol. ii, pp. 399–400.

tence will result in greater happiness, on balance, than his valet's. The valet's son or brother is entitled to consider his own anguish as an item, and a very large item, in the hedonic calculus. But he is wrong to allow his vivid appreciation of this one item to blind him to the greater suffering of others, when that is involved. Godwin did not really revise his opinion about this; but he was worried in case he had given the impression that the affections did not matter. That was not his meaning. Justice and love are not finally opposed, though they may be on occasions in an imperfect world. So far as possible, we should remodel the world so that the conflict will not occur. That is why he comes down on the opposite side when considering pardons. Punishment is a human institution: and human institutions can be remodelled. If you have to choose between Fénelon and your father, choose Fénelon; but you ought to try to save both. If you have to choose between the individual and society you may have to choose society; but we cannot remain satisfied with a society that presents us with the choice.

The conflict between justice and love, between the individual and society, between my own happiness and the general happiness: these are the problems with which Godwin is faced in 'the famous fire cause'. They are the central problems for morals and politics. Godwin may not have solved them; but at least he saw the weaknesses of the contemporary solutions. The magic word 'sympathy' will not solve the conflict between egoism and altruism: my sympathy and affection for my father, the valet, may militate against the general happiness instead of contributing to it. Nor is it enough to say that, since I am a member of society, self-love and the love of society are, in the last analysis, the same. Saving Fénelon will, *ex hypothesi*, be for the good of society, and, as a member of society, I will share in that good; but it would be absurd to suggest that this will compensate me for my personal loss. Nor can we trust to a divinely implanted moral sense, secure that, if only I follow it, I will automatically do whatever makes for the greatest happiness of the greatest number. The impulse to save my father has the fullest support of the moral sense, if by the moral sense we mean simply an immediate intuitive approval. If by the moral sense we mean our reason when applied to right and wrong, then it yields us only the greatest happiness principle itself. There is no short cut which will tell us intuitively what makes for the greatest happiness.

Godwin, then, arrives at the utilitarian solution, at about the same time as Bentham, and apparently independently of him. But his utilitarianism is free from the inconsistencies in which both Bentham and Mill entangled themselves, inconsistencies which, it is often said, were not plainly seen by anyone before Sidgwick. Godwin, though quite as thoroughgoing in his application of the greatest happiness principle as Bentham, saw plainly enough that it could not be based on egoistic hedonism. Partly for this reason, Professor Priestley denies[1] that Godwin was a utilitarian at all, and suggests that he was merely using the utilitarian formulas without really meaning them; his position was 'essentially that of Shaftesbury and Hutcheson, and of the Greek tradition', while in some respects he is even closer to Price. The question is partly a verbal one. If utilitarianism is defined as including egoism and relativism, Godwin was not one; neither was Sidgwick, and it is doubtful if even Mill was. But it seems to me that Godwin went much further than Shaftesbury or Hutcheson. He opposed natural rights, including the right to property, on the grounds that we have no right to anything except what will make for the greatest happiness of the greatest number. He opposed the social contract theory on the ground that promises are not the basis

[1] In his edition of *Political Justice* (University of Toronto Press, 1946), iii. 15–16.

of morality, but are indeed essentially opposed to it. Anything
I promise will either make for the general happiness, or
against it. In the first case the promise is unnecessary, and in
the second case it is wrong. He said of punishment that 'an
innocent man is the proper subject of it if it tend to good; a
guilty man is the proper subject of it under no other point of
view'.[1] He summed up his moral theory in just two sentences:
'The end of virtue is to add to the sum of pleasurable sensation. The beacon and regulator of virtue is impartiality, that
we shall not give that exertion to procure the pleasure of an
individual, which might have been employed in procuring the
pleasure of many individuals.'[2] This principle of impartiality
was his nearest approach to the moral sense: it is not essentially different from Bentham's 'every one to count as one, and
no one for more than one'. He did indeed, like Sidgwick,
regard it as an ultimate moral principle, which could not be
deduced from egoism. But it is at least arguable that Godwin
was not a confused and half-hearted utilitarian, but an exceptionally clear-sighted one, who has been much neglected
by the historians of utilitarianism.[3]

2

'The voluntary actions of men originate in their opinions.'
This sentence occurs as a kind of refrain throughout the
Enquiry. Godwin himself obviously regarded this as the most
valuable of the 'new, true and important ideas'[4] by means of
which he was anxious to reform the world. It has been seized

---

[1] *P.J.* ii. 327.   [2] *P.J.* ii. 493.

[3] It is interesting to notice that a contemporary pamphlet attacking
Godwin treats *Political Justice* as the *reductio ad absurdum* of the greatest
happiness principle. See *An Examination of the Leading Principle of the
New System of Morals* (&c.) (London, 1798). The pamphlet is anonymous,
but it was generally known that the author was Thomas Green, of
Ipswich.

[4] Preface to *Caleb Williams* (Routledge, 1903), p. xix.

on by his critics as the central fallacy of all his thinking. Godwin, it is said, was a closet philosopher, a professorial politician who thought he could make men virtuous by arguing with them. He reached the pinnacle of absurdity when he suggested (though tentatively) that the truly virtuous man might be able to restrain his intending murderer by the mere force of reason. 'The powers of reason and truth are yet unfathomed.' Godwin, it is said, must of course be excused for not having read Freud or Marx; but the merest acquaintance with the affairs of the world might have taught him that men are creatures of passion and impulse far more than of reason. He must, as Leslie Stephen suggests, have been 'a quiet and amiable dreamer', able 'to ignore all inconvenient facts', whose 'opinions were too deeply rooted in abstract speculation to be upset by any storms raging in the region of concrete phenomena'.

Godwin was less innocent of the world than has been supposed. The 'summary of principles' at the beginning of *Political Justice* includes this:

The voluntary actions of men are under the direction of their feelings.

Reason is not an independent principle, and has no tendency to excite us to action; in a practical view, it is merely a comparison and balancing of different feelings.'

Godwin had read Hume and was well acquainted with the view that reason is the slave of the passions. He gives it, indeed, a qualified assent. He had not read Freud, but he fully realized the possibility of rationalization. ('Nothing is more usual than for a man to impute his actions to honourable motives, when it is nearly demonstrable that they flowed from some corrupt and contemptible source. On the other hand many persons suppose themselves to be worse than an impartial spectator will find any good reason to believe them.')[1]

[1] *P.J.* i. 63.

He had not read Marx, but one of his principal objects is to show that men's characters and actions are determined by the structure of society.

What becomes, then, of his repeated assertion that the voluntary actions of men originate in their opinions? And how can they be also 'under the direction of their feelings'?

Desire, Godwin admits, is in some sense the source of all action. 'The things first desired by every thinking being will be agreeable sensation, and the means of agreeable sensation. If he foresee anything that is not apprehended to be pleasure or pain, or the means of pleasure or pain, this will excite no desire, and lead to no voluntary action.'[1]

This seems complete psychological hedonism. But the emphasis is on the word *first* in the first sentence. Godwin immediately goes on to modify the doctrine by introducing the principle of association of ideas as laid down by Gay and Hartley. He uses the classic illustration of the miser who, desiring money originally as a means, comes to prize it for its own sake. 'Something of this sort happens very early in the history of every passion.' Benevolence is in this respect no different from avarice. 'The good of my neighbour could not, in the first instance, have been chosen, but as the means of agreeable sensation.' But, like wealth, or fame, or the drunkard's craving, it speedily becomes a motive in its own right.

But at this point Godwin introduces a fresh consideration. 'Thus far', he says, 'there is a parallel nature in avarice and benevolence. But ultimately there is a wide difference between them. When once we have entered into so auspicious a path as that of disinterestedness, reflection confirms our choice, in a sense in which it never can confirm any of the factitious passions we have named.'[2]

In what sense can reflection confirm our choice? Godwin

---

[1] *P.J.* i. 424.   [2] *P.J.* i. 427.

seems to mean that the greatest happiness principle, or something like it, is immediately apparent to reason.

We find by observation that we are surrounded by beings of the same nature with ourselves. They have the same senses, are susceptible of the same pleasures and pains, capable of being raised to the same excellence, and employed in the same usefulness. We are able in imagination to go out of ourselves, and become impartial spectators of the system of which we are a part. We can then make an estimate of their intrinsic and absolute value; and detect the imposition of that self-regard, which would represent our own interest, as of as much value as that of all the world beside.[1]

The principle of impartiality, then, is an axiom of reason. But it directly contradicts the principle of self-interest, to which our actions must, by an inexorable psychological law, conform. Does this mean that man, though capable of seeing the better course, is inevitably doomed to choose the worse?

There were two main arguments by which Godwin's contemporaries tried to avoid this conclusion.

1. First, you could call in God to rectify the imperfections of man. God alone was capable of being motivated by the principle of impartiality. But He would see to it that the selfish impulse of men had beneficial results. He would do this very simply by a system of rewards and punishments after death. All that men needed to realize was that they would attain happiness by doing the will of God. Since God is benevolent, it follows that His will is that we shall be benevolent too.

Godwin will have none of this solution. To do the right action for the wrong reason, he says, is not to be virtuous.

If self-love be the only principle of action, there can be no such thing as virtue. Benevolent intention is essential to virtue. . . . We may be made indeed the instruments of good, but in a way less honourable than that in which a frame of wood, or a sheet of paper,

[1] *P.J.* i. 427.

may be the instruments of good. . . . In this sense, we may admire the system of the universe, where public utility results from each man's contempt of that utility, and where the most beneficial actions, of those whom we have been accustomed to term the best men, are only instances in which justice and the real merits of the case are most flagrantly violated. But we can think with little complacence of the individuals of whom the universe is composed.[1]

It is partly because of these sentiments that Professor Priestley denies that Godwin was a utilitarian. And indeed this position does seem hard to reconcile, not merely with Godwin's utilitarianism, but with his determinism. Why should Godwin object to a theory which made man less honourable than a frame of wood, since he himself believed that 'the assassin cannot help the murder he commits, any more than the dagger'?

I am not sure that Godwin is completely consistent here. But his main position about virtue is fairly clear. Virtue resides in the motive; but that does not mean that it is good except as a means. My duty is to do whatever does as a matter of fact make for the general happiness, not what I think will make for it. 'Was it the duty of Everard Digby to blow up King James and his parliament with gunpowder? Certainly not. Duty is the application of capacity to the real, not imaginary, benefit of mankind.'[2] The application of capacity, Godwin adds, is a concept equally applicable to inanimate objects. A knife has a capacity for cutting, and this may or may not be applied to the benefit of mankind. 'Duty is a species under this generical term, and implies merely the best application of capacity in an intelligent being.'[2]

But when we talk of virtue, as distinct from duty, we consider motives as well as consequences. An action is virtuous when it 'proceeds from kind and benevolent intention' and also has 'a tendency to contribute to general happiness'. Both

[1] *P.J.* i. 433-6.　　　　　　　　　[2] *P.J.* i. 157.

criteria are necessary. Why should the first be brought in at all? Why not allow an action to be virtuous if it contributes to the general happiness, whatever the motive of the agent? Because, Godwin would say, we regard the action not merely as it is in itself, but as a cue to the probable future actions of the agent. The wild shot of an incompetent marksman may happen, by a lucky chance, to hit the target. We would say, however, that it was not really a good shot, and we would say this without implying that there is some transcendental goodness about a shot that has no relation to its efficiency in hitting the target. This is not Godwin's illustration; but I think he does mean that the motive of benefiting mankind is the only virtuous motive because it is the only reliable motive.

This is evident in what he says about punishment. In punishing, we inquire into the motive of the offence; but this is quite compatible with punishing according to the harm done to the community.

Shall we inflict on the man who, in endeavouring to save the life of a drowning fellow creature, oversets a boat, and occasions the death of a second, the same suffering, as on him who, from gloomy and vicious habits, is incited to the murder of his benefactor? In reality, the injury sustained by the community is by no means the same in these two cases; the injury sustained by the community is to be measured, by the anti-social dispositions of the offender....[1]

The virtuous motive is not, however, completely reliable. Godwin has an eloquent passage on the harm that good men do. 'The most determined political assassins, Clement, Ravaillac, Damiens and Gerard, seem to have been deeply penetrated with anxiety for the eternal welfare of mankind. For these objects they sacrificed their ease, and cheerfully exposed themselves to torture and death. Benevolence probably had its part in lighting the fires of Smithfield, and pointing the daggers of Saint Bartholomew.'[2] He concludes that: 'Intention no doubt is of the essence of virtue. But it will not do alone. In deciding of the merits of others, we are bound, for the most part, to proceed in the same manner as in deciding the merits of inanimate substances. The turning-point is their utility. Intention is of no further value than as it leads to utility: it is the means, and not the end.'[1]

What this means in practice is that two things are needed for virtue: benevolent intention, because without it there can be no real assurance of benevolent actions; knowledge, because without that benevolent intention may still fail of benevolent results.

This raises another of the grounds on which it can be doubted whether Godwin was a consistent utilitarian. Professor Priestley suggests that he values, not only virtue, but also knowledge and truth, for their own sakes. As a psychological statement about Godwin, this may very well be true: but he would himself have said that knowledge and sincerity, though of the utmost importance, are, like virtue, means and not ends. The real point is that Godwin has no faith in lucky accidents. The wrong motive may occasionally result in the right action, but in the nature of things this is not likely to happen often. Similarly ignorance and deception may occasionally enable us to blunder on to the right path, but we cannot rely on this. Seeing things as they are, and revealing our knowledge frankly to others, is much more likely to yield us results in the long run: though Godwin knew well enough that the run might be very long indeed. Ultimately, his conviction about this was possibly a matter of faith: it implied a belief in a very different kind of universe from Paley's. Godwin did not believe in a God who manipulated events so that indirect routes would lead to the goal of desire. Man could only attain to the general happiness by his own efforts: and it was necessary first that he should want to attain it, and

[1] *P.J.* i. 156.

secondly, that he should discover and take careful note of the relations between phenomena, including the phenomena of his own mind. In all this, as in his final conclusions about the nature of generalization, Godwin is curiously close to Spinoza.

These, then, are Godwin's main grounds for objecting to 'theological utilitarianism', the doctrine of eternal rewards and punishments as a mediating factor between egoism and universalism. He opposes it mainly on the assumption that it is in fact untrue, and known to be untrue by those who propagate it. They do so because they think it is necessary to impose on the mass of mankind in order to make them virtuous. Here Godwin is content to argue that the deception must fail. The actual connexion of events in the world round us cannot fail to impress the mind; in spite of all the prejudice and ignorance in the world, the logic of facts has some effect on us.

But all that can be told me of a future world, a world of spirits, or of glorified bodies . . . is so foreign to everything with which I am acquainted, that my mind in vain endeavours to believe, or understand it. If doctrines like these occupy the habitual reflections of any, it is not of the lawless, the violent and the ungovernable, but of the sober and conscientious, overwhelming them with gratuitous anxiety, or persuading them passively to submit to despotism and injustice, that they may receive the recompense of their patience hereafter. The objection is equally applicable to every species of deception. Fables may amuse the imagination; but can never stand in the place of reason and judgment as the principles of human conduct.[1]

He is, however, inconsistent in also suggesting that, if the doctrine were true, it would be immoral. The argument that the virtuous motive is the only reliable motive would not apply if a God did manipulate events so as to make private vices

[1] *P.J.* ii. 127–8.

result in public benefits. And, in that case, there would be no real reason, on utilitarian principles, to call them vices at all. In saying that we would then admire the system of the universe, but not the individuals in it, Godwin is not adhering to his own conception of virtue. But this is, I think, a minor inconsistency.

2. But the stock utilitarian solution of the problem stated on page 18 was worked out by David Hartley. Hartley's general argument has two main steps. First, it depends mainly on chance whether a man takes pleasure in this thing or in that thing: in the love of his fellow men or in torturing stray cats. More specifically, it depends on the associations, or, as a later generation would put it, on the conditioned reflexes he happens to have formed in the course of his life. It follows that if a celestial or mortal Jeremy Bentham wants him to take pleasure in whatever makes for the greatest happiness of the greatest number, his job is to see that the right associations are formed. This is a surer way than the method of rewards and punishments, because there is now no inducement to obtain the reward without earning it. Virtue now becomes its own reward.

For Hartley, however, the associations between our own happiness and the general happiness are not entirely factitious. It is here that the second step in the argument comes in. The pleasure which comes from these associations, it is argued, is actually more pleasant than that which comes from different associations. In one sense pleasure is purely subjective: you take pleasure in something if that happens (as the result of your past history) to be the sort of thing you like. But it is an objective fact, Hartley claims, that if you had been so conditioned as to like a different kind of thing, your total pleasure would have been either greater or less. The reason for this is that some associations fit together better than others. If you form the elaborate set of associations that results in your taking pleasure in wife-beating, you are necessarily cut off from some other kinds of marital pleasure. And so on. This is of course simply the 'integration' theory of ethics, of which Hartley is probably the father.[1]

We have, then, two senses in which self-love and the love of society may be said to be the same. They will be the same for you if you happen to associate your own greatest pleasure with the well-being of others. You may be brought to form this association (strictly this set of associations) by subjection to the group *mores*, which is of course a process of conditioning. If, on the other hand, you have formed a different set of associations, your interest and that of the community will not coincide. Membership in any community, whatever the *mores*, will not in itself be enough to ensure that the requisite associations are formed. It would seem, then, that self-love and the love of society are the same in some communities but not in others.

If, however, we ask which community the egoist would choose to live in, the answer is that he would choose the one in which men are led to identify their own interest with that of others, because this leads to a way of life which is better integrated, and so ultimately more satisfying than any other. In this sense self-love and the love of society are the same in all communities.

The obvious objection to this is that private and public interest plainly do, on occasion, conflict. What are we to say, for example, of the martyr? Hartley would not say, certainly, that the martyr gets more pleasure from his martyrdom than from any alternative course of action, or even that he thinks he will. He would agree that the martyr does not think of

---

[1] Cf. Godwin: 'It (vice) is followed in most instances by remorse; or, when it is not, remorse is only excluded by a certain hardness and brutality of temper, which is solitary in its character, and incompatible with genuine delight.' *Life of Geoffrey Chaucer* (London, 1803), i. 310.

pleasure at all. What he does say is that in his (largely unconscious) pursuit of pleasure the martyr has formed the habits of choice that make him, in a particular set of circumstances, choose martyrdom just as the miser may be led to prefer money to the things that money can buy, for the sake of which he first learned to love money. But the miser is plainly being foolish. Are we, then, to say the same of the martyr? I think Hartley would say that the martyr's habits of choice, unlike the miser's, really do make, on the whole, for a fuller and more satisfying life. If, in particular circumstances, they lead to disaster, that is a risk which he has to take, and which is worth taking. But might he not draw back and abandon his principles at the point at which it becomes clear that they make martyrdom inevitable? Would not this be the wise, and, for an egoist, the right course? I think Hartley (who was, let us remember, a determinist) would say that it is not a possible course. It would be possible only if the martyr's habits of choice had not been quite wholehearted: if there had always been present a vacillating tendency which would itself tend to make him less a whole man, and so less happy. There is a sense, then, in which we can say that the martyr's life, considered as a whole, is happier than it would have been if he had not been a martyr. But this is not the same as saying that the martyrdom, considered in isolation, is his greatest possible pleasure.

For Hartley, then, the moral sense arises out of a particular set of associations. As the result of the accumulated experience of a given community, certain types of action become associated, rightly or wrongly, with the approval of other men ('ambition'), the blessing of God ('refined self-interest'), the possibility of having friendly relations with one's fellows ('sympathy'), the possibility of feeling at one with the universe ('theopathy'). These actions are called 'right'. And, like the love of money, the desire to do right actions, arising at first as a means, becomes an end in itself. When that happens, the moral sense has come into existence.

In a sense it depends on convention: to act morally is to do something because it is right, and what is thought to be right depends largely on the *mores* of the community. But the *mores* themselves embody a (possibly confused) conception of what makes for the greatest good of the agent. One is tempted to say that the individual grows in moral insight in proportion as he comes to realize the connexion between right action and personal happiness, and so departs from the *mores* when he finds them to be confused. But for Hartley 'realize' and 'insight' are not the right words. We do not see the connexion through reason: in almost a literal sense, we feel it in our bones. The connexion, that is to say, is impressed on us, on our nerve centres, on 'the white medullary substance of the brain', through experience. Since the connexions are physiological, we cannot say that they may be true or false; but they may be more or less integrated, more or less 'consistent with one another, with the frame of our natures, and with the course of the world'. In so far as they are integrated, the individual will in fact attain the greatest good of which he is capable. In that sense morality is objective. But we pass from a lesser to a greater integration, not through a process of reason, but through being subjected to the right kind of experience. Participation in the *mores* of the community forms a large part of this experience, but not the whole of it. It is possible to achieve a different systematization from the one embodied in the *mores*; but one does not simply reason one's way out of them.

Godwin retained a good deal of all this; enough to prevent the 'reason' he extols from being the passionless, abstract, bloodless faculty most of his critics have thought it. But he did feel it necessary to free Hartley's system 'from the scheme of material automatism with which it was unnecessarily clogged'.

Moral development, he would say, does not end at the point where Hartley leaves it. To act morally is not merely to act from the motive of doing one's duty: this should be reinforced by a rational insight into the nature of duty. This insight should be generated from the moral sense, much as the moral sense itself, in Hartley's scheme, is generated from sympathy, theopathy, 'gross self-interest', and the rest.

But what, precisely, will we see into? On Hartley's principles, the answer would seem to be: into the connexion between right action and our own greatest happiness. For Godwin the answer is: into the connexion between right action and the greatest happiness of the greatest number. But how is it possible to maintain that the moral sense, the habit of associating certain types of action with various sources of happiness for ourselves, should lead to an insight, not into the nature of those connexions, but into a connexion with something quite different? The short way out of this difficulty is by the route of Bentham and Mill. It is implicit in Hartley's analysis that (not indeed the actions but) the dispositions that make for the happiness of the individual also make for the general happiness. Godwin accepts this, at least as a general rule. Why not then say that an insight into the nature of duty will also involve the knowledge of this happy coincidence as well? The famous equation (psychological hedonism = ethical egoism = utilitarianism) is then complete.

Godwin did, I think, toy with this solution. But there is a difficulty. It is, I suggested, open to Hartley to say that the martyr acts only from the motive of doing his duty, but that he has cultivated the disposition which leads him so to act as the result of a largely unconscious search for pleasure, and that the disposition is of value because it does in fact make for his greatest possible pleasure, not as a direct result of the act of martyrdom, but in the quality of life which the disposition makes possible. But this position is possible for Hartley only because he leaves rational insight out of account. Once suppose that the martyr is fully conscious of the connexion between duty and self-interest, and we can hardly deny that self-interest is in fact his conscious motive. Moreover, it would now seem possible for him, after all, to draw back at the point where it becomes obvious that the path of duty and of self-interest no longer coincide. That is the difference between saying that our actions result from feelings which owe their psychological development and their emotional force to their connexion with self-interest, and saying that they result from reasoning about self-interest.

Godwin, then, is driven to adopt a different solution. What he says is briefly this. We are incapable, in the first instance, of desiring anything except as a means to our own pleasure. But that leads us to desire to understand ourselves and our surroundings, if only in order to control them. In gaining understanding we come also to see that our own happiness has no claim to be preferred to anyone else's. We come to see this because it is in some sense a fact, an axiom to be grasped by reason. It may be compared with another principle of reason, that we must accept the conclusion to which the evidence points. Godwin accepts this, not as an ideal, but as a fact about the structure of our minds. If we have really grasped the premises, we cannot but assent to the conclusion. We may contrast this with what happens when we rationalize. Here we assent to a conclusion, not because the evidence points to it but because we want to accept it on quite other grounds.

For Godwin the principle of impartiality is implicit in reason in much the same way. We cannot understand the universe unless we see 'things as they are' (the sub-title, it will be remembered, of one of Godwin's novels).[1] But to see

---

[1] *Caleb Williams, or Things as they are.* In the early editions it was called *Things as they are, or The Adventures of Caleb Williams.*

things as they are is necessarily to feel certain emotions towards them. Knowledge is impossible unless we can bring ourselves to adopt 'the scientific attitude', the impartial, objective viewpoint. You cannot, for instance, investigate disease unless you free yourself, in part at least, from horror of it, and regard it coolly as just one of the possibilities inherent in living tissue. It is a condition of reason that it is impartial, just as it is a condition of reasoning that you follow the argument whithersoever it leads. Neither principle can be proved: they are not, in that sense, facts. But we can hardly reason unless we adopt both of them: to exercise our reason is indeed to adopt them. It is not so much that we draw conclusions about values from the facts, as that we are not in a position to learn the facts unless we adopt an attitude that does affect our value judgements. 'What magic is there in the pronoun 'my' that should justify us in overturning the decisions of impartial truth'?

There is here a question for the determinist. Our actions, says Godwin, are determined by our opinions, and our opinions are themselves determined. But are they determined by the principle of reason, by the force of facts, by our inability to dissent from the conclusion once we have really grasped the premises, or are they determined by our desires, by such mental processes as rationalization?

I think Godwin's answer is that our actions are determined, at least in the first instance, by desire. But they are also determined by reason; it is true that once we have grasped the premises, we cannot but assent to the conclusion. All that is necessary is that we should, in the first instance, have sufficient incentive to exercise our reason. We have this incentive since in general desire prompts us to increase our understanding of things as they are. Once we have formed the habits of mind inseparable from the exercise of reason, we may well follow courses of action that conflict with desire. As reasoning beings, we cannot do otherwise, provided that we have really grasped the premisses. But this does not mean that rationalization is impossible. Desire may very well hinder us from grasping the premisses; and the obstacle may sometimes be insuperable. That is why it is important that society should, through its institutions, provide us with every possible incentive to see things as they are. The exercise of reason will not indeed lead men to see that their own interests and those of others coincide; because, although this is true in general, it is not always true. What is necessary is that self-interest should lead men to pursue reason to the point where understanding, at first desired as a means, becomes an end in itself. Once it becomes an end in itself, the principle of impartiality, which is implicit in reason, cannot but assert itself.

We have, then, the paradox that egoism transcends itself. Godwin accepts psychological hedonism as modified by Hartley's associationism, but rejects egoism in favour of utilitarianism. His position is not without its difficulties. We will not, he says, fully do our duty unless we are able to reason about it, and to reason about duty is not to reason about self-interest. It is, on the contrary, to reason about the greatest happiness of the greatest number. Yet he also says that this can become a motive for us only because of associations with self-interest. We are to become fully conscious of the connexion between right actions and the general happiness (and so correct our notions of what actions are right), but not, it would seem, of the connexion between the general happiness and our own happiness. Or perhaps we are to be conscious of the general connexion, and to be motivated by that consciousness, and yet persist in considering the general happiness even when (as in 'the famous fire cause') it becomes obvious that the general happiness conflicts with our private and personal happiness.

This seems an impossible position. Perhaps, indeed, it is: it seems unlikely that psychological hedonism is finally compatible with a reasoned utilitarianism. But two points can be made. First of all, if Godwin made a mistake here it was because he was trying to avoid the mistake of which he is generally accused. He realized the importance of the emotional springs of action. (He was indeed able to say quite flatly that 'moral reasoning is nothing but the awakening of certain feelings'.[1]) He knew that reason must have its appetitive side. He was attracted to Hartley because he seemed to explain how this was possible. When he found that the explanation consisted in denying reason altogether, he tried to amend it. If he did not solve the problem, at least it can be said in his defence that it is not easy to solve.

Secondly, it is unfair to say that Godwin's moral philosophy is a mere *pastiche*: that he took bits from Price, from Hartley, from Hutcheson, from Hume, from Helvétius, from Adam Smith, without bothering to reconcile them. He did work out a detailed and quite subtle reconciliation. Whether or not it is finally satisfactory, it deserves more consideration than it has had. At the very least, it should have earned him a more honourable place in the history of utilitarianism.

3

I have quoted Godwin's dictum that 'moral reasoning is nothing but the awakening of certain feelings'. Feelings are not, however, best awakened by exhortation; they come of themselves provided we have sufficient knowledge.

Let us take an example. I may readily agree that it is a bad thing that millions of Asiatics should be starving, and that I ought to do something about it. But in practice I probably won't. We are inclined to say that this is because my purely

---

[1] *Memoirs of Mary Wollstonecraft*, 1798 (Constable, 1928), p. 89.

intellectual apprehension of the facts is not reinforced by any emotional apprehension of them. But now suppose that an Asiatic comes and starves on my doorstep. Almost certainly I shall be moved to feed him. Again it seems reasonable to say that the sight of his sufferings touches my emotions as the mere abstract knowledge of them does not. But more than this is involved. When I see a man starving before my eyes, the proposition: 'starvation ought to be relieved' takes on a new meaning for me. I can now see in detail precisely how and why starvation is bad; I can see exactly how the generalization applies to the particular instance. It is not a question of perfect knowledge being reinforced by emotion; my knowledge before was imperfect. When it becomes perfect, it necessarily brings the emotion with it: it is no longer possible for desire and emotion to conflict.

Generalizations, then, are inadequate as a guide to the emotions. It is only when we apprehend the particular instance in the light of the generalization that the appropriate emotions are kindled. The distinction is the one Spinoza makes between *ratio* and *scientia intuitiva*. Godwin insists that 'reason' does not stop with general principles (and he is speaking specifically of moral principles).

It would be preposterous to suppose that, in order to judge fairly, and conduct myself properly, I ought only to look at a thing from a certain distance, and not consider it minutely. On the contrary, I ought, as far as lies in my power, to examine everything upon its own grounds, and decide concerning it upon its own merits. To rest in general rules is sometimes a necessity which our imperfection imposes on us, and sometimes the refuge of our indolence; but the true dignity of human reason is, as much as we are able, to go beyond them, to have our faculties in act upon every occasion that occurs, and to conduct ourselves accordingly.[1]

We can now, I think, see why 'the famous fire cause' was

[1] *P.J.* i. 345.

crucial for Godwin, why he wanted to write a treatise on morals in order to correct the false impression he had made in his handling of that problem. He intended to explain and clarify, not to recant. He did not want to advocate a bloodless reason that turned its back on the human affections. There should be no conflict between the greatest happiness principle and the affections. We should not stifle them in trying to follow the tight-lipped axioms of morality, general rules in which we see only from a distance. The point is that we should have as vivid an apprehension of the sufferings of the rest of humanity as of those of our dearest friends. So far from wishing to sacrifice emotion to reason, Godwin wants reason to be charged with emotion. The greatest happiness principle must become the passion of universal benevolence. But we do not achieve this by bringing in emotion as something extraneous to reinforce reason: we must perfect reason itself. When we really see something clearly, instead of 'looking at things from a distance', the appropriate emotion comes of itself.

We have already seen the application of this to Rousseau's dilemma about pardons. If benevolence and justice appear to conflict, it is because the benevolence is not true benevolence, or (and this is more likely) because the justice is not true justice. It is for that reason that Godwin approves of the small self-governing community. If a man is to be judged, let him be judged by his friends and neighbours, who know him intimately. They will see his case in its true inwardness: they will be in no danger of applying rules of thumb, which ignore all the circumstances that make every case unique. To understand all is to pardon all; but if we pardon because we understand, the pardon and the judgement do not conflict. We do not commit the absurdity of saying with one breath: 'it is right that you should be punished', and with the next: 'I shall graciously, in my clemency (that is to say, rightly) refrain from punishing you.'

It is not, then, reason, but only the rule of thumb, that conflicts with the emotions. That is why Godwin objects so strongly to rules of thumb. 'He that believes the most fundamental proposition through the influence of authority does not believe a truth, but a falsehood. The proposition itself he does not understand, for thoroughly to understand it is to perceive the degree of evidence with which it is accompanied; is to know the full meaning of the terms, and by necessary consequence to perceive in what respects they agree or disagree with each other.'[1]

If we interpret his 'reason' in this way, what Godwin says about virtue becomes more intelligible and more consistent. Virtue is good only as a means to the general happiness; on the other hand, the right action is the one that results from a virtuous disposition. Godwin's point is that the man who does what he mistakenly believes to be his duty is not fully virtuous: at best he is only following rules of thumb; and, since his knowledge is at fault, his disposition is at fault also. A virtuous disposition consists, after all, in feeling the right emotions: in recoiling in horror from cruelty, in sympathizing with affection, and so on. The man who, from a mistaken sense of duty, assassinates a tyrant or burns a heretic at the stake or condemns a murderer to the gallows is not feeling the appropriate emotions. He does not really understand the tyrant or the heretic or the murderer; he does not see how their actions follow from their past history and present circumstances. If he did, he would feel towards them only charity. In Spinoza's language, the passive emotions of 'righteous indignation' and so forth would be transformed into the active emotion which comes with understanding.

In the long run, the general happiness can only be attained if all men feel the right emotions. They are hindered chiefly by

[1] *P.J.* ii. 184.

the need, in a large and complex society, of general principles as 'resting-places for the mind'. Hence the first step to virtue is to remodel society so that men will be able to see 'things as they are'. It is, paradoxically, the implications of 'the famous fire cause' that finally led Godwin to renounce the reign of law in favour of anarchism.

2

REASON AND FEELING

I

GODWIN'S predecessors had disputed whether reason or feeling was the basis of morals. It is usual to regard Godwin as the supreme apostle of reason. But actually he wavered between the two schools of thought; and in the end he is closer to Hutcheson or Hume than to Clarke or Price. The problem seems to have worried him a good deal. He went out of his way to revise *Political Justice* in order to insert, in the third edition, the statement quoted in the last chapter about reason being the slave of the passions. And, in his diary for 1798, he recorded his intention of writing a book, to be called *First Principles of Morals*, in order 'to correct certain errors in the earlier part of my *Political Justice*. The part to which I allude is essentially defective, in the circumstance of not yielding a proper attention to the empire of feeling.'[1]

We have already seen the causes of this uncertainty. The greatest happiness principle, and the principle of impartiality, the two basic principles on which Godwin's moral philosophy depends, are in some sense axioms of reason; and it is only by appealing to their reason that men can be induced to act virtuously. On the other hand virtue consists, essentially, in feeling the appropriate emotions.

The truth is that Godwin does not sufficiently distinguish between feeling an emotion and seeing that it is the right emotion. He tells us that 'the voluntary actions of men originate in their opinions', and that these opinions are opinions about what is good or desirable. But this assertion

[1] C. Kegan Paul, *William Godwin: his friends and contemporaries* (London, 1876), i. 294.

depends, I think, on a confusion between thinking something desirable and desiring it.

It is true that Godwin seems to distinguish between these two, for he says that to think something desirable is to necessarily to desire it; and this is not to say that the two are identical, but simply that, as a matter of psychology, one always accompanies the other. But when we ask for the proof of this assertion, we find that it does depend, after all, on identifying the two. A voluntary action, says Godwin, is accompanied by foresight of the consequences: 'the hope or fear of a certain event is its motive'; that is what distinguishes it from an involuntary action. He goes on:

The mind decides 'this is good' or 'desirable'; and immediately upon that decision, if accompanied with a persuasion that we are competent to accomplish this good or desirable thing, the limbs proceed to their office. The mind decides, 'this is better than something else'; either wine and cordials are before us, and I choose the wine rather than the cordials; or the wine only is presented or thought of, and I decide that to take the wine is better than to abstain from it. Thus it appears that in every voluntary action there is preference or choice, which indeed are synonimous terms.[1]

This is Godwin's proof of his primary principle that 'the voluntary actions of men originate in their opinions'; and he argues from this both that to think something desirable is to desire it, and that to desire something is to think it desirable. But he is not really entitled to say more than that 'the voluntary actions of men originate in their desires', a proposition which few would dispute. In the passage quoted above he should have said: 'The mind decides "this is what I desire", and immediately . . . [&c.]. The mind decides, "I desire this more than I desire something else"; either wine and cordials . . . [&c.].' The passage is plausible only if 'good' and 'desirable' mean 'desired', and 'better' means 'desired more'.

[1] *P.J.* i. 58.

Once the distinction between 'desired' and 'desirable' is made, it is obvious that Godwin has no grounds at all for what he is saying. He has certainly not proved that to desire something is to think it desirable, or vice versa; throughout he has simply assumed this.

We can find further evidence of this in Godwin's answer to the obvious objection, that men do often choose things which they recognize to be undesirable. They may, says Godwin, recognize this on reflection, but not at the moment of choice. 'It may happen that the opinion may be exceedingly fugitive; it may have been preceded by aversion and followed by remorse; but it was unquestionably the opinion of the mind in the instant at which the action commenced.'[1] And if anyone says, with Ryle, that he can decide that smoking is undesirable at the very moment of lighting his pipe, Godwin's reply is that he does not really think it undesirable; he is merely repeating a rule of thumb; he does not understand the evidence on which it is based; he has no vivid apprehension of the evil consequences of smoking. The argument is very like the familiar one that the strongest desire always conquers. If anyone points to a negative instance, the answer is: 'It couldn't really have been the strongest desire.' There is no proof of this except that it failed to conquer; and it is obvious that 'the strongest desire' is taken to mean 'the desire that conquers'. Similarly Godwin does not really distinguish between thinking something desirable and desiring it.

Now this confusion really stems from psychological hedonism. Men desire pleasure. To call something 'good' or 'desirable' is to call it pleasant. This is not quite the same thing as to say that it is desired; for men may not realize that it is pleasant. To say 'this is desirable' is to say 'this is pleasant, and you would desire it if you realised how pleasant it

[1] *P.J.* i. 58.

was'. It is impossible for anyone to realize that something is pleasant and not to desire it; for men are not constituted like that. But of course he can repeat somebody else's judgement that 'this is pleasant' without fully realizing why the judgement was made.

If anyone asks: 'But is pleasure really desirable, really good?' he is indulging in meaningless mumbo-jumbo. That pleasure is good is ultimately a biological fact: a feeling rather than a proposition, and a feeling that men cannot but have.

I think that this is the argument that is really at the back of Godwin's mind in the passage I have quoted. But it cannot come to the front of his mind, because he has rejected egoism in favour of utilitarianism. He continues to say (with Locke):

Good is a general name, including pleasure, and the means by which pleasure is procured. Evil is a general name, including pain, and the means by which pain is produced. Of the two things included in these general names, the first is cardinal and substantive, the second has no intrinsic recommendations, but depends for its value on the other. Pleasure therefore is to be termed an absolute good; the means of pleasure are only relatively good. The same observation may be stated of pain.[1]

Good, then, is pleasure. But not, Godwin insists, merely our own pleasure. The doctrine that we can desire only pleasure becomes, for him:

'The voluntary actions of men are under the direction of their feelings; nothing can have a tendency to produce this species of action, except so far as it is connected with ideas of future pleasure or pain to ourselves or others.'[2]

The words 'or others' change, if they do not destroy, the whole position. That our own pleasure is good can be regarded as ultimately a feeling rather than a proposition: a

---

[1] *P.J.* i. 440. And see Locke's *Essay*, bk. ii, ch. 20.
[2] Godwin's MS. notes published in Paul, *William Godwin*, i. 294.

fact about ourselves, not about the external world. It is another way of saying that man is motivated by self-interest. But it is by no means so plausible to say that we cannot but desire the pleasure of others. The meaning of 'desirable' has been radically changed; and if we now go on insisting that to see that something is desirable is necessarily to desire it we are asserting, not psychological hedonism, but human perfectibility.

Godwin was not alone in making the transition. He had authority in Shaftesbury, in Hutcheson, and even in Butler. The psychological hedonist had dismissed as meaningless the question: 'Is self-interest really good?' His answer might be put by saying that self-interest carries its own authority along with it. Butler retorted that conscience, too, carried its own authority along with it, quite as obviously as self-interest. As a *tu quoque*, this had its force; but it provided no reason for preferring conscience to self-interest, if the two should conflict. Butler was indeed driven to say that the two were co-ordinate principles, and that in the final analysis they never do conflict. Shaftesbury, who wanted to say that benevolence carried *its* own authority along with it, was faced by the same difficulty. To say that man is moved solely by self-interest is to say that he feels that his own interest is to be preferred to any alternative. To say that he is also moved by benevolence is to say that he feels that the interests of others are to be preferred to at least most alternatives. If self-interest and benevolence pull him in different directions, how is he to decide between them? Hutcheson tried to solve the problem by postulating a third feeling, the moral sense, which had the special function of making the decision. Butler, Shaftesbury, and Hutcheson are all of them extending the egoist argument that the first premiss of ethics, the ultimate value judgement on which all others depend, is simply a biological fact about human beings. It just is a fact that man is moved by self-interest, and it is quite meaningless to ask whether he ought to be. It is quite natural to reply that man is also moved: (a) by benevolence, (b) by the conviction that he ought to prefer benevolence to self-interest. But if the moral sense is just one feeling among others, why should it have any special authority? Because it is itself a conviction that some feelings should be preferred to others? But self-interest (i.e. self-interest as a motive or disposition, selfishness as we would more naturally call it, self-love as it was commonly called) may be regarded as itself a conviction that my own pleasure should be preferred to the pleasure of others. If the moral sense is the opposite conviction, then we can only say that men are torn by conflicting feelings: the question cannot be, Which feeling is right? but only, Which feeling is the stronger? But once the argument is put on this plane, the advocates of self-interest would seem to have an easy victory. Butler, Shaftesbury, and Hutcheson were all of them inclined to dodge the issue by saying that self-interest and the moral sense do not really conflict, in the long run. Indeed, they were inclined at times to concede the whole egoist position by turning the moral sense into just another source of pleasure, the pleasure of a satisfied conscience, to be balanced against the more obvious physical pleasures. Hartley does take this line, quite explicitly.

There are two ways of avoiding this impasse. One is to say, with Price, that the moral sense cannot be just one feeling among others: the faculty that is to judge between the feelings cannot be itself a feeling. This raises the whole problem of how reason can move to action, and how value judgements can be justified by reason. The other is to say boldly, with Godwin, that benevolence is stronger than self-interest, after all: or at least that it would be, if men knew all the facts.

This appeal to knowledge of the facts is again derived from egoism. If men are moved solely by self-interest, then the problem of choosing between alternative courses of action is simply the problem of discovering which course will give us the greater pleasure. And this is the kind of question which reason is fitted to decide. We do need the value judgement: 'the greater pleasure is always to be preferred to the lesser'; but this can be, plausibly enough, regarded as part of what is meant by the basic assumption that man is moved by self-interest. We may, out of short-sightedness, prefer the immediate small pleasure to the remote greater one; but it is at least plausible to suppose that we could not do so if we really understood how and why the remote pleasure was greater. The conclusions to which reason leads us will, indeed, be put in the form of value judgements: 'This is good' or 'This is better than that'. But these are to be interpreted: 'This causes pleasure' or 'This causes more pleasure than that'; and these are questions of fact. Ultimately only one value judgement is involved: 'Pleasure is good' and its corollary 'The greater pleasure is to be preferred to the lesser'; and these are guaranteed, not by reason, but by instinct.

Reason, accurately speaking, [says Godwin] has not the smallest degree of power to put any one limb or articulation of our bodies into motion. Its province, in a practical view, is wholly confined to adjusting the comparison between different objects of desire, and investigating the most successful mode of attaining those objects. It proceeds upon the assumption of their desirableness or the contrary, and neither accelerates nor retards the vehemence of their pursuit, but rather regulates its direction, and points the road by which we shall proceed to our goal.[1]

This position is only tenable so long as we suppose that man has, at bottom, only one instinct. Reason may arbitrate between desires by referring them to that instinct; but if there are two instincts, self-love and benevolence, what then? Hutcheson, as we have seen, does not really help matters by

[1] Godwin's MS. notes, quoted in Paul, *William Godwin*, i. 294.

postulating a third instinct, the moral sense. Apart from the other difficulties, his moral sense does not seem to differ from benevolence itself. He says that its function is to arbitrate between self-love and benevolence; but it would seem to be a singularly partial judge. All its decisions are in favour of one side.

> In those cases where some inconsistency appears between these two determinations, the moral faculty at once points out and recommends the glorious the amiable part. . . . It recommends the generous part by an immediate undefinable perception. . . . And thus, where the moral sense is in its full vigour, it makes the generous determination to publick happiness the supreme one in the soul, with that commanding power which it is naturally destined to exercise.[1]

From this passage it would be quite reasonable to conclude that the moral sense is nothing but the greatest happiness principle itself, i.e. the conviction that we ought to do whatever makes for the greatest happiness. But just as self-love can be regarded as the conviction that we ought to do whatever makes for our own happiness, so benevolence can be regarded as just this opposing conviction. At least it can be so regarded if we suppose that there is a principle of 'universal benevolence' parallel to 'cool self-love'. According to Butler, cool self-love enables us to choose between conflicting self-regarding impulses. Its basic principle is that the greater pleasure is to be preferred to the lesser. It is not quite clear whether Butler postulates a similar faculty to arbitrate between particular benevolent impulses. But Hutcheson does, quite specifically. And once again the regulating principle will be: the greater pleasure is to be preferred to the lesser.

Now, although it may be convenient to distinguish between cool self-love and a particular selfish impulse, both are really manifestations of the same basic instinct, self-interest.

[1] Francis Hutcheson, *System of Moral Philosophy*, 1755, i. 77.

If cool self-love regulates the particular desires, this is merely another way of saying that the instinct regulates itself. Hutcheson argues that benevolence regulates itself in exactly the same way, making use of Shaftesbury's distinction between 'entire' and 'partial affection'. If a judge on the bench feels so much pity for the prisoner that he closes his eyes to the effects on other, innocent people of not restraining him, he is the victim of a partial affection. But if his benevolent feelings towards the community as a whole modify his attitude to the prisoner, then we have an 'entire', or, as Shaftesbury also calls it, a 'proportionable' affection. It can be described as pity for the prisoner and pity for his victims each given its due weight; but it is not that some superior faculty judges between two separate feelings of pity. The more extensive pity drives out the lesser.

Hutcheson seized on this as an answer to the objection that the faculty that judges between two feelings cannot itself be a feeling. Feeling, he said, corrects itself: it is not corrected by reason. But Shaftesbury had said that the partial affection 'has no Foundation or Establishment in Reason'; and Price, when he comes to make the same distinction as Shaftesbury, talks about 'rational benevolence' and 'instinctive benevolence'. The same distinction reappears in Godwin, in Price's form rather than Hutcheson's:

Philanthropy, as contradistinguished to justice, is rather an unreflecting feeling, than a rational principle. It leads to an absurd indulgence, which is frequently more injurious, than beneficial, even to the individual it proposes to favour. It leads to a blind partiality, inflicting calamity, without remorse, upon many perhaps, in order to promote the imagined interest of a few. But justice measures by one unalterable standard the claims of all, weighs their opposite pretensions, and seeks to diffuse happiness, because happiness is the fit and proper condition of a conscious being.[1]

[1] *P.J.* i. 323.

This looks like reason controlling the passions, after all. And probably Godwin did think of it like that: he seems to have vacillated between Price's position and Hutcheson's. The passions are to be controlled by the principle of impartiality, and Godwin does think of that as an axiom of reason. But it could be argued that the principle of impartiality is a corollary of universal benevolence just as 'the greater pleasure is to be preferred to the lesser' is a corollary of self-interest. If a man is really moved by self-interest, he only needs to see that pleasure A is greater than pleasure B and he will prefer it. If pleasure A is remote and only to be attained by patient effort, and pleasure B is within easy reach, it may take self-control to reject B in favour of A; and this can be described as reason regulating desire. But really you don't need to bring in something else to control self-interest; self-interest, if sufficiently 'enlightened', will control itself. In precisely the same way, if benevolence makes me seek X's happiness (the happiness of my mother the chambermaid, for example) and Y's happiness is greater than X's, benevolence itself will make me prefer Y's. The same elements in my nature that make X's happiness important to me, as a result of my close sympathy with her, will make Y's happiness equally important, if I could attain the same close sympathy with him. Before I can prefer pleasure A to pleasure B, I need something more than the mere belief, as a rule of thumb, that A is greater than B: I need the same vivid apprehension of tomorrow's pleasure that I naturally have of today's. In the same way, I need the same vivid apprehension of a stranger's happiness that I naturally have of my friend's. But reason is well fitted to provide me with this vivid apprehension; for it is to be achieved by exposure to a greater range of experience, by knowledge, in the full sense of knowledge, of more facts. 'Enlightened' self-interest is merely a more complete self-interest; 'rational' benevolence is merely a more complete benevolence. Each can be called 'entire' as opposed to 'partial'. In this way it is possible to maintain Godwin's essential position and still say that reason 'is wholly confined to adjusting the comparison between different objects of desire'. It is this movement of thought, I would suggest, that is behind his vacillation on this point.

But this position is only tenable if we suppose that man is at bottom actuated by only one instinct: either self-interest or benevolence, but not both. Otherwise we are faced with the problem of deciding between them, when they conflict. Why should one instinct have more authority than any other, unless we mean that it is stronger than any other? Godwin, I have suggested, took the heroic course of saying that benevolence is stronger than self-interest. But perhaps it would be more accurate to say that he reversed the egoist argument. The egoist reduced benevolence to self-interest; in a sense, Godwin reduced self-interest to benevolence. At least we can say that this is a possible development from the argument we have just considered, about entire and partial benevolence.

For in this argument we have already taken the crucial step of treating A's happiness as of equal importance with B's. For 'entire' self-interest to drive out partial self-interest, we merely need to concede that twenty units of pleasure for ourselves is better than one unit. For entire benevolence to drive out partial benevolence we have to say that the pleasure of twenty people is better than the pleasure of one person. The two assertions are superficially alike: indeed either may be meant by the ambiguous statement that the greater pleasure is to be preferred to the lesser. But of course the difference is important. It is just here that we have what is perhaps the basic difficulty of utilitarianism.

Now once this step has been taken, it becomes possible to absorb self-interest in benevolence. To realize that A's happiness is as important as B's, even though A is a stranger and B a close friend, it is only necessary to have the same intimate knowledge of A that I now have of B. Of course this is impossible in practice. At least it is impossible to know all the A's as well as I know B. In practice, Godwin later admitted, this may even be a good thing, on the division of labour argument. But the principle remains. And just as I always know my friend better than a stranger, so I always know myself better than I know even my friends. We need then look no farther for an explanation of the partiality we all feel for ourselves. There are not, after all, two warring instincts in human nature, each stubbornly opposed to the other. If entire benevolence can drive out partial benevolence (in principle: never completely in practice) then it can also, at least in principle, drive out self-interest, which is indeed merely one form of partial benevolence. We do not need to alter human nature; all we need is greater knowledge, at least of the kind that makes for sympathetic understanding. And, as we have seen, self-interest itself gives us the incentive to increase our understanding of other human beings. As our understanding increases, we cannot but be convinced of the principle of impartiality. At least we will have some glimmering of it, and with fuller understanding our conviction will grow.

There are, however, two difficulties, closely connected. First, there does seem to be an important difference between saying that twenty units of happiness to ourselves is better than one unit, and saying that the happiness of twenty people is better than the happiness of one. Demonstrate to someone that he will be happier if he does X rather than Y, and, if he really believes this, he will not merely say: 'yes, that's right', he will feel an impulse, at least at the moment, to do X. But many people would say that, although they see the reasonableness of saying that the happiness of a hundred must be preferable to the happiness of one, they feel no urge to promote the happiness of mankind in general as distinct from the happiness of their friends and families. Butler may have been right in his hesitancy about supposing a feeling of universal benevolence, as distinct from particular generous impulses to particular people. The principle of impartiality, unlike the corresponding principle about our own pleasure, seems to be something we think, not something we feel.

But this would mean that we cannot, after all, say that human beings are at bottom benevolent, in the way that the egoists say that they are at bottom selfish. We can only say that they ought to be benevolent. In one way the difference may be more apparent than real. The egoist does not say, after all, that men always do pursue their own greatest pleasure in the long run, as distinct from the pleasure of the moment: only that they can be made to see that they ought to. But the conviction that they ought to rests ultimately on feeling, not on reason: on self-interest itself. It is not so clear that the conviction that we ought to prefer the general happiness to the happiness of a few also rests on feeling, on benevolence itself.

It is because of this difficulty, I think, that Godwin is unclear about the exact status of the principle of impartiality; I think this is why he vacillates between the school of reason and the school of feeling. I do not mean that he was fully conscious of the difficulty, or that it presented itself to him in quite this way. It is simpler to say that he was impressed both by Hutcheson's arguments and by Price's, and that he never bothered to reconcile them. But some appreciation of this problem does, I think, lie behind his inconsistency. At least my interpretation explains why Universal Benevolence and the Principle of Impartiality were both important to him, and why they were closely connected in his mind. It also shows how these beliefs arose quite naturally out of psychological hedonism and the attempts of Butler, Shaftesbury, and Hutcheson to combat it.

2

Whether the greatest happiness principle and the principle of impartiality are ultimately guaranteed by feeling or by reason, Godwin's main thesis is unaffected. The way to improve men's behaviour is to increase their knowledge. It is not quite true that virtue is knowledge; virtue, Godwin says explicitly, 'may be defined to promote the happiness of intelligent beings in general'.[1] But it is impossible not to feel this desire once we see things as they are. There seem to be two steps in this argument: (*a*) to see things as they are is to see what is desirable, (*b*) to see what is desirable is to desire it.

So far I have suggested that Godwin simply assumes (*b*); and that in doing so he was influenced by the egoist argument that any judgement of the form '*x* is desirable' means '*x* is pleasant or the cause of pleasure'. The only value judgement involved is 'pleasure is desirable', and this is reducible to the biological fact that all men desire pleasure. But it can also be argued that (*b*) follows once we understand what is meant by (*a*).

There is a passage in Hume which illustrates very well what Godwin meant by seeing things as they are. If while safe on land we are thinking about those in peril on the sea, we may, Hume points out, either feel pleasure at our own superior position or sympathetic pain at their inferior one. But, he goes on, 'suppose the ship to be driven so near me that I can perceive distinctly the horror painted on the countenance of the seamen and passengers, hear their lamentable cries, see the dearest friends give their last adieu, or embrace with a resolution to perish in each other's arms: no man has so savage a heart as to reap any pleasure from such a spectacle, or withstand the motions of the tenderest compassion and sympathy.'[2]

[1] *P.J.* i. 316.
[2] Hume, *Treatise*, bk. iii, pt. 3; ed. Selby-Bigge (O.U.P. 1896), p. 594.

With Hume the emphasis is not merely on the emotional force of a vivid impression. He is talking about the conflict between sympathy for others and complacency about ourselves.

We judge more of objects by comparison, than by their intrinsic worth and value; and regard every thing as mean, when set in opposition to what is superior of the same kind. But no comparison is more obvious than that with ourselves. . . . This kind of comparison is directly contrary to sympathy in its operation. . . . The direct survey of another's pleasure naturally gives us pleasure; and therefore produces pain when compared to our own. His pain, considered in itself, is painful; but augments the idea of our own happiness, and gives us pleasure.[1]

We may therefore actually rejoice in the suffering of the sailors when we contemplate it from a distance; but this attitude can hardly survive a nearer view. And this may be compared with a passage in Godwin's novel *Mandeville*.

Abstractions and generalities are subjects of our moral reasonings: while we contemplate them, we are conscious of a certain elevation, that is flattering to the mind of man; but it is only through the imagination, and when we apply our reflections to an individual, when the subject upon which our thoughts are occupied, comes before us clothed in flesh and blood, and presents a set of features and a sensible reality, that our passions are roused through every fibre of our heart.[2]

Seeing things at a near view, then, affects both our opinion of what is desirable and our desires. The two are fused and can hardly be separated.

But why then, it may be asked, does Godwin put all the emphasis on the opinion and none on the desire? If he means that a desire for *x* and an opinion that *x* is desirable are fused, so that we can hardly distinguish them, why does he say that

---

[1] Hume, *Treatise*, ed. Selby-Bigge, pp. 593-4.
[2] Godwin, *Mandeville* (Edinburgh, 1817), iii. 45-46.

our voluntary actions originate in our opinions, not (as we would more naturally say) in our desires? The answer is, of course, that he has in mind another set of opinions as well: not only our opinions about what is desirable, but our opinions about what is the case. The appeal to reason is not primarily an appeal to 'abstractions and generalities': it is an appeal to the facts. We are to correct the distant view by means of the near one.

But there is still a gap in the argument. It is reasonable to suppose that, if we examine all the facts and examine them at close quarters, the resulting opinion will be the right one. But can we say that the resulting emotion will be the right one? 'The right opinion' means the true opinion; but what is a right emotion? It is tempting to say that the emotion which arises out of a true opinion is a right emotion, but of course this need not follow. If all men feel compassion when they see what is really involved in a shipwreck, this may just be a universal human weakness. If 'the right emotion' means anything, it does not mean the emotion which men in fact feel when they know the full facts: it means the emotion they ought to feel.

It is to bridge this gap that Godwin needs the dogma of human perfectibility. He does not mean that human beings are perfect, or that they will ever become perfect. The difficulties in the way of ever knowing the full facts may be insuperable. Nevertheless, improvement is always possible, because knowledge, though necessarily incomplete, can be increased without limit. But this does not mean that knowledge always will increase, or that its growth in one direction may not be counter-balanced by the growth of prejudice in another direction. Godwin would have agreed, I think, that in his own time the Industrial Revolution was multiplying new causes of prejudice. His belief in human perfectibility must not be identified with the Victorian belief in progress.

Why, then, does he insist on it so much? Because he needed it as a fundamental hypothesis for his ethics: it is the hypothesis that the emotions men feel when they know the full facts are the right emotions. That this is no more than a hypothesis is obscured by talking, not about emotions or desires, but about opinions that something is desirable; for it seems obvious that the opinions that men form when they know the full facts must be the right opinions.

That is why Godwin prefers to talk about 'opinions' instead of desires or feelings. But he does not deny, when pressed, that an opinion that something is desirable is really a feeling. The important point is that it is a feeling that we cannot help having when faced with certain facts. When we succumb to present temptation, it is because some of the facts are not present to our minds. At the moment of acting, we may be said not to know them.

One of the fallacies by which we are most frequently induced to a conduct which our habitual judgment disapproves, is that our attention becomes so engrossed by a particular view of the subject, as wholly to forget, for the moment, those considerations which at other times were accustomed to determine our opinion. In such cases it frequently happens, that the neglected consideration recurs the instant the hurry of action has subsided, and we stand astonished at our own infatuation and folly.[1]

The obvious objection to this is that we do not, in any ordinary sense of the word, forget these considerations at all. As Ryle points out, 'I frequently persuade myself to smoke less, filling and lighting my pipe at the very moment when I am saying 'yes' to the conclusion of the argument'. And, to an imaginary objector, who says (as Godwin would certainly have done) 'Ah, but you weren't "really" or "effectively" convinced', he retorts 'Certainly. This proves that unwisdom

[1] *P.J.* i. 62.

in conduct cannot be defined in terms of the omission of any ratiocinations.'[1]

What it proves, Godwin would have said, is that being able to recite a generalization is not the same as knowing the particulars which are subsumed under it. Ryle comes fairly close to this in the distinction he makes between the 'museum-possession' and the 'workshop-possession' of knowledge. I may, he says, be able to reel off a list of road distances for places between Oxford and Henley, as I can reel off the multiplication table,

But if, when told that Nettlebed is so far out of Henley, I cannot tell you how far Nettlebed is from Oxford, or if, when shown a local map, I can see that Oxford to Banbury is about as far as Oxford to Henley but still cannot tell you how far Oxford is from Banbury or criticise false estimates given by others, you would say I don't know the distance any longer, i.e., that I have forgotten it or that I have stowed it away in a corner where it is not available.[1]

It is in this sense that Godwin would say that we 'forget' the considerations that would make us stop smoking even if we can recite them at the moment of lighting up. He would agree with Ryle that more is involved than 'ratiocination', if that is confined to deductive inference; but he would not agree that there is some special kind of knowledge, 'knowing how', that is distinct altogether from 'knowing that'. We do not 'effectively know' a generalization unless we can see in detail how it applies to any given particular. I do not know (in this sense) that smoking is bad for my health unless I know precisely what aches and pains will result and how they will affect me; I do not know that shipwrecked sailors suffer unless I know in detail the horror on their faces, their last farewells, and so on. The generalization is indeed a shorthand expression, a 'resting-place for the mind' comprising a

[1] G. Ryle, 'Knowing How and Knowing That', in *Aristotelian Society Proceedings*, xlvi (1946), 1–16.

multitude of such particulars. To know *how* to apply the generalization is to know that the generalization applies to a particular case in such-and-such a manner; but this is part of the meaning of the generalization, and can be fairly described as 'really' or 'effectively' knowing the generalization itself.[1]

All errors in conduct, then, can, according to Godwin, be traced to some error in belief. The error in belief will probably, however, be of a rather curious kind. All voluntary actions, Godwin says, may be taken as evidence of an opinion: '*X* is good, or desirable'. But, in the first place, our actions are seldom perfectly voluntary. They are almost always done partly from habit. And, secondly, propositions like '*X* is good' are, on Godwin's showing, fairly complex. He gives us as an example a man going to church.

He goes partly for the sake of decorum, character, and to secure the good will of his neighbours. A part of his inducement also perhaps is, that his parents accustomed him to go to church at first, from the mere force of authority, and that the omission of a habit to which we have been formed is apt to sit awkwardly and uneasily upon the human mind. Thus it happens that a man who should scrupulously examine his own conduct in going to church would find great difficulty in satisfying his mind as to the precise motive, or proportion contributed by different motives, which maintained his adherence to that practice. It is probable however that, when he goes to church, he determines that this action is right, proper or expedient, referring for the reasons which prove this rectitude or expediency, to the complex impression which remains in his mind, from the inducements that at different times inclined him to that practice.[2]

'Going to church is desirable', then, may mean: (*a*) I will be conforming to custom if I go to church, (*b*) the neighbours

---

[1] Spinoza makes the same point by saying that we are not certain of the generalization, though we do not doubt it. *Ethics*, ii. 49, schol.

[2] *P.J.* bk. i, ch. 5, vol. i, pp. 66–67.

will be friendly to me if I go to church, (c) Father will punish me if I don't go to church. And it may mean several other things as well. Some of these propositions ((c), for example) are no longer true, and others need qualification. The church-goer would probably realize this if he explicitly formulated them to himself. The opinions, then, on which voluntary action is based may be ones which the agent is not conscious of holding and to which he would not assent if they were put to him.

It will be seen that Godwin is less of an intellectualist than is generally supposed. His position so far is not very different from Hume's. We learn to feel approval for actions which are associated in our minds with pleasure for ourselves or for others. Our choice of action is based primarily on these habits of feeling, and only secondarily on the beliefs which give rise to them. He goes on, however, to argue that it is possible to change these habits of feeling by making the beliefs explicit and examining them. When we do this, we find that our sentiments have been based on a very incomplete survey of the relevant facts. If we take all the facts into account, we will realize that our actions have other consequences in the way of causing pleasure or pain to ourselves or others; and this will rouse in us new sentiments of approval or disapproval. Our final considered choice will be for that action which makes for the greatest happiness of the greatest number; since, as we have seen, we cannot help preferring this once the full consequences are really present to our minds.

But it is of course impossible to make a complete calculation of the hedonic consequences of each and every action. We cannot avoid general rules of conduct; most of our choices are, and must be, habitual.

Perhaps no action of a man arrived at years of maturity is, in the sense above defined, perfectly voluntary; as there is no demonstration in the higher branches of the mathematics, which contains the whole of its proof within itself, and does not depend upon former propositions, the proofs of which are not present to the mind of the learner. The subtlety in the human mind in this respect is incredible. Many single actions, if carefully analysed and traced to their remotest sources, would be found to be the complex result of different motives, to the amount perhaps of hundreds.[1]

Godwin goes on immediately to remark that 'the perfection of the human character consists in approaching as nearly as possible to the voluntary state'. But I do not think he means that human beings are ever likely to be able to dispense with routine habits of choice. What he advocates is: (1) that the habits of choice which we acquire as members of a community should be based, as far as possible, on a full consideration of the facts, and not, as is usual, on a partial consideration of them; (2) that we should also acquire the habit of questioning even these attitudes and of varying them as circumstances dictate.

Both these ends are most easily attained in the small, self-governing community, where generalizations are likely to be based on a real apprehension of particulars.

[1] *P.J.* i. 68.

GODWIN AND MONTESQUIEU

AMONG the terms of abuse showered on Godwin and his supporters, there is one that recurs constantly. It is curiously mild and is at first sight rather puzzling. The word I mean is 'abstract'.

There are, I think, three distinct charges hinted at by this apparently colourless word. It means, in the first place, something like 'highbrow'. There is the suggestion of a sneer at *all* political theory, simply because it is theory. We see this attitude clearly in the words put in Godwin's mouth by the author of *St. Godwin*:

... with a terrible pother about what nobody could understand; namely; the *absoluteness of necessity*, the *perfectibility of man*, and the *omnipotence of truth*, I opposed all political and moral order, and endeavoured to overturn every system that time and experience had sanctioned and approved.[1]

This is simply the conservative's dislike of any academic inquiry into the prevailing *mores*.

Secondly, the word means something like 'starry-eyed'. Godwin, it is suggested, was full of his own dreams of the ideal society. Living in this dream world, he was quite blind to reality. As Leslie Stephen put it, he was 'too deeply rooted in abstract speculation to be upset by any storms raging in the region of concrete phenomena'.

This is the common complaint of the 'practical' (i.e. conventional) man against the 'idealist'.

But the third charge is the most important. Godwin and his like, it is said, created an entirely fictitious 'human

[1] Edward Dubois, *St. Godwin, by Count Reginald de St. Leon* (Dublin, 1800), p. 216.

nature'. Friends of humanity, they cared little for mere men. A contemporary satirist said of *Political Justice*:

The first trait of the work is, a certain cold-blooded indifference to all the mild, pious and honourable feelings of our common nature, like all the Philosophers of the new Sect. The next thing observable, is a most affectionate concern and regard for the welfare of mankind, who are to exist *some centuries hence*, when the *endless perfectibility of the human species* (for such is their jargon) shall receive its *completion* upon earth. . . .[1]

There are two versions of this charge. Sometimes it is said, as here, that Godwin's theory of human nature is simply false; sometimes the complaint is that he has appealed to 'human nature' at all. But the two complaints are usually combined. For, it is said, to consider what all men have in common is to ignore the extent to which men are moulded by society. 'Nature' in 'human nature', as in 'the state of nature', is contrasted with 'society'. To appeal simply to human nature is to create an asocial monster that never existed; for, while all men belong to some community, no one community is quite like another. Men may be expected to differ, then, in almost all the traits that they owe to society. It is, then, a vicious abstraction to speak of 'man' at all; in a sense there are no men, but only Englishmen or Frenchmen or Hottentots.

So far our account of Godwin may seem to substantiate this charge. It is all very well, it may be said, to talk about 'appropriate' emotions which man cannot but feel if they see things as they are. Actually, this is dubious, even in theory: it is by no means certain that there are 'right' emotions in the sense that there are accurate judgements of size or colour. At any rate it is certain that in practice men's emotions are the direct result of the society in which they live. They may

[1] T. J. Mathias, *The Pursuits of Literature; a satirical poem in four dialogues*, 9th ed., 1799, p. 210 n.

be regarded as a 'function' of the economic, political, legal, and social institutions. Anthropology, it is claimed, has demonstrated this beyond doubt. There is little point in asking whether the emotion which a Polynesian feels for his chief, or for a tapu building or artifact, is or is not 'appropriate'. It is appropriate for him, both in the sense that he cannot but feel it, and in the sense that the emotion is bound up with a complex set of beliefs and attitudes that affect every part of his life. Often enough, it is said, an emotion may have its origin in a belief that is no longer consciously held. In our own society respect for royalty and for rank dates from a political and social system that has been transformed beyond recognition. The old attitudes survive, not through mere inertia, but because the existing institutions have their roots in the past, and could not continue to function unless supported by at least some vestiges of the attitude of mind that brought them into being. We talk about the British, or the American 'way of life'; but a way of life is not something that can be mastered by learning a set of principles, like a mathematical method. It consists in particular ways of doing things, and particular ways of feeling about things. Any particular practice or attitude can be 'explained' only historically. But the whole complex, if not a rational unity, is very much a unity in practice. Condemn this attitude or that as 'inappropriate', demand that it be renounced in the name of reason, and you will find unexpected consequences in some apparently unrelated field of behaviour.

Burke was the great exponent of this view in the eighteenth century. And Burke, it is commonly said, laid his finger on the central fallacy of the whole school of Jacobin reformers.

You see, Sir, that in this enlightened age I am bold enough to confess, that we are generally men of untaught feelings; that instead of casting away all our old prejudices, we cherish them to a very considerable degree, and, to take more shame to ourselves, we cherish them because they are prejudices; and the longer they have lasted, and the more generally they have prevailed, the more we cherish them. We are afraid to put men to live and trade each on his private stock of reason; because we suspect that this stock in each man is small, and that the individuals would do better to avail themselves of the general bank and capital of nations and ages.[1]

The delicate fabric of society, in short, is woven of prejudice. Gradually, without deliberation, as a result of simply taking the next step forward as it presented itself, we have built up a social structure and a corresponding set of attitudes. The individual fits into the social structure because he shares the attitudes; start tampering with them, with the best intentions in the world, and the whole of society may collapse. No doubt it is irrational to bend the knee to a mere man because he happens to bear the name of someone who was honoured by a king several centuries before; but in the mind of the average citizen, if not in your mind, respect for rank is bound up with doing his duty to his fellow men. Again, it may be unreasonable for John Jones to refrain from beating his wife because of the superstitious beliefs of the inhabitants of the Near East more than 2,000 years ago; but we had better be thankful for the fact and not try to interfere with a faith that has such beneficial results. But, you say, his duty to his wife rests on quite other grounds, and it would be better for him to know them. Perhaps it would, but for him the grounds are religious: it will be easier for you to destroy his beliefs than to give him new ones. 'Prejudice', says Burke, 'renders a man's virtue his habit; and not a series of unconnected acts. Through just prejudice, his duty becomes a part of his nature.'

It is easy to see why this third sense of 'abstract' should be combined, in the popular mind, with the other two. For here,

[1] Edward Burke, *Reflections on the French Revolution and other essays* (Everyman ed., London, 1910), p. 84.

it would seem, we have a philosophic justification of the conservative's dislike of change and the conventional man's distrust of theory. It was now possible to say, not merely that people like Godwin were dangerous meddlers, but that all such meddling was fundamentally wrong, because it ignored the fundamental facts about the structure of society and man's place in it. The reformers, it was said, lacked 'the historical approach'.

What is usually overlooked in all this is that Godwin himself was far from denying that man is moulded by society. It was no part of his creed that human nature was unalterably fixed. On the contrary, that doctrine was one of the stumbling-blocks in his path. 'You can't change human nature' is the cry, not of the starry-eyed reformers, but of the 'practical' man who likes to think that his feet are firmly on the ground. It was raised in the eighteenth century by Tories like Hume; and Godwin thought he could answer them precisely because he saw the importance of social influences on men's thoughts and actions. He puts this, indeed, in the forefront of his whole system: in the first chapter of his book.

Perhaps government is, not merely in some cases the defender, and in others the treacherous foe of the domestic virtues. Perhaps it insinuates itself into our personal dispositions, and insensibly communicates its own spirit to our private transactions. Were not the inhabitants of ancient Greece and Rome indebted in some degree to their political liberties for their excellence in art, and the illustrious theatre they occupy in the moral history of mankind? Are not the governments of modern Europe accountable for the slowness and inconstancy of its literary efforts, and the unworthy selfishness that characterises its inhabitants? Is it not owing to the governments of the East that that part of the world can scarcely be said to have made any progress in intellect or science?

When scepticism or a spirit of investigation has led us to start these questions, we shall be apt not to stop at them. A wide field of speculation opens itself before us. If government thus insinuate itself in its effects into our most secret retirements, who shall define the extent of its operation? If it be the author of thus much, who shall specify the points from which its influence is excluded?[1]

But, it may be said, this is merely the other side of the same medal. If you believe that human nature is bad, then of course you will say that reform is impossible. But if you believe that human nature is good, as the Jacobins did, then you will of course blame all existing human defects on society. You will, then, be ready to embrace the doctrine that society moulds the individual. But you will think of this process as essentially one of corruption; you will still be uninterested in man as moulded by society, that is, in man as he is. You will turn away from the living men all round you, with their passions and their prejudices and their patriotism, to the quite imaginary vision of man as he might be if only he could be cleansed of this social pitch. You will still, in short, be guilty of 'abstraction'.

Now it is true that the notion of man as naturally good, and corrupted only by society, is not entirely absent from Godwin's thought. 'Naturally good' means, for him, that men will inevitably feel the appropriate emotions if only they see things as they are. There is nothing especially visionary about this theory: it is not very different from what Hutcheson had said. Certainly Godwin does not advocate the return to 'natural man' and the simple life in the way that some of Rousseau's followers did. In *Mandeville* he has put an eloquent defence of these views (they are Rousseauist, though not quite Rousseau's) into the mouth of Clifford, who, while still at Winchester, expounds them to an enraptured audience of his schoolfellows:

Well, [he would say] I am destined to be poor. And what is poverty? As long as my blood flows cheerily in my veins, and a

<hr>

[1] *P.J.* i. 4–5.

light heart dimples in my cheeks, I shall be the truly enviable man. I know some will tell me riches are the genuine means of independence and liberty. But it is all a cheat. The rich man is the only slave. He cannot move without scores of menials to attend him. He cannot dine without twenty dishes before him. . . . He calls himself the master of all these and he is the slave of all. He cannot go forth, and take the air, until his servants please. He is at the mercy even of his horses. . . . Upon what an accumulation of circumstances does the tranquillity of every day of his life depend! How is every climate under Heaven searched and put under contribution, before his slightest meal can be supplied! And, if the minutest of these circumstances goes wrong, how is your fancied god immediately turned into a wretch! . . . He is the truly independent man that has truest wants. . . . Every state and clime will supply him with what he needs. . . . Nor is he the slave of any habits or indulgencies. What he had to-day, he can dispense with to-morrow. . . . I have heard it said, If the rich man could but know the miseries and agonies of pain, the anguish of heart, and the dreadful paroxysms of despair, that are going on, perhaps in the next street to that which his lordly palace occupies, he would find but little relish in his dainties. But I wish that were the worst of it. He is not only the neighbour of misery; but he is the author of unnumerable instances of it.[1]

This goes on for pages. Godwin, though he represents Clifford's companions as enchanted by these views, obviously has some doubts about his readers. 'Set down in cold lines and paragraphs, they may appear long-winded and pedantic.'[2] But the interesting thing is that Mandeville himself expressly dissents from these views:

I was strongly impressed with the notion of their fallacy. . . . I confessed to myself that wealth was pregnant with mischief, both to the possessor, and to society in general. But I did not look upon poverty with the same views as Clifford did. I saw that man is not formed like the animals, to whom uncultivated nature

[1] *Mandeville* (Edinburgh, 1813), i. 239–43.   [2] Ibid. i. 253.

supplies every want. . . . I saw that in civilized society, the only
state that appeared to me worthy of man, he could not subsist but
upon the fruits of others' industry or of his own, and that the
attempt to supply himself subjected him in various ways to the
caprice of his fellow-creatures, and was in various ways precarious.
I saw that the poor man was strangely pent up and fettered in his
emotions, whether their purpose might be to unfold the treasury
of intellect in the solitude of his closet, or to collect facts and
phenomena by wandering on the face of the earth. . . . I saw that,
if riches made a man a slave, entire poverty did the same, and
perhaps more effectively. . . . I saw that poverty was environed on
all sides with temptations, urging and impelling a man to sell his
soul, to sacrifice his integrity, to debase the clearness of his
spirit, and to become the bond slave of a thousand vices.[1]

There is a question of interpretation here. *Mandeville* is
written in the first person; but Mandeville is not normally
to be identified with Godwin. Mandeville is that typical
Godwin figure, the victim of his own prejudices. He is
jealous of Clifford, and his jealousy leads him to misunder-
stand and persecute him. Normally, then, Clifford is in the
right and Mandeville in the wrong; or, putting it another
way, Godwin approves of Clifford's actions and opinions,
and disapproves of Mandeville's. But this need not apply to
every speculative opinion Clifford advances; and it is fairly
clear that on this question of poverty Mandeville is for once
Godwin's mouthpiece. For the same point of view appears
elsewhere: for example, in *St. Leon*.

I put in my claim for refinements and luxuries; but they are the
refinements and purifying of intellect, and the luxuries of un-
costly, simple taste. I would invite the whole world, if I knew how
to do it, to put in a similar claim. I would improve my mind; and
I would enlarge my understanding; I would contribute to the
instruction of all connected with me, and to the mass of human
knowledge. The pleasures I would pursue and disseminate, though

[1] *Mandeville*, i. 256–7.

not dependent on a large property, are such as would not be understood by the rustic and the savage.[1]

And in the *Life of Chaucer* Godwin, not this time speaking through a fictitious character, but in his own person, says something not very unlike Hobbes:

The savage is a grave character; his mode of existence is too insecure and he is too often called upon for sudden and unforeseen exertion, not to maintain in him inflexibly this temper of mind. The barbarian, in proportion as he recedes from this primitive condition of man, feels himself more secure and at his ease, dismisses his gloom, and is at leisure to cultivate a sort of rude vein of jocularity and sport.[2]

Godwin, then, does not simply say: away with civilization! He does not hold up the peasant or the savage as the exemplar of natural goodness. Refinements and luxuries are necessary if goodness is to be cultivated; and poverty corrupts no less than wealth.

Nevertheless, he would agree that men have been, in a sense, corrupted by civilization. It is, after all, society that prevents them from seeing things as they are. Their prejudices get in the way; and prejudices, as we have seen, result from rules of thumb. But rules of thumb are necessary in any society, and particularly in large and complex societies. The point has been well put by R. H. Tawney:

The most crucial and the most difficult of all political questions is that which turns on the difference between public and private morality. The problem which it presents in the relation between states is a common-place. But, since its essence is the difficulty of applying the same moral standard to decisions which affect large masses of men as to those in which only individuals are involved, it emerges in a hardly less acute form in the sphere of economic

[1] *St. Leon* (London, 1799), i. 229.
[2] William Godwin, *Life of Geoffrey Chaucer* (London, 1803), i. 57.

life, as soon as its connections ramify widely, and the unit is no longer the solitary producer, but a group. . . . Granted that I should love my neighbour as myself, the questions which, under modern conditions of large-scale organization, remain for solution are, Who precisely *is* my neighbour? and, How exactly am I to make my love for him effective in practice?[1]

This is one way in which society creates prejudice. Dealing with men in large groups, we can no longer see them as individuals. We think of them as landowners and tenants, as capitalists and workers, even as men and women (the New Woman or the Mere Male) and not as John Jones or Mary Smith. We can hardly deal with human beings without generalizing about them; but every generalization, when applied to an individual, is to some extent false. And the cumulative effect of many such slight errors is the mass of misunderstandings which divide human beings. The judge on the bench, for example, is no longer capable of seeing the poor wretch before him for what he is; he deals with him simply as a 'case', as one instance of a class of offenders. His legal maxims apply (more or less) to the class; they may have little relevance to the individual. So far, then, from dealing exclusively in abstractions, Godwin sees existing society as necessarily confused by abstractions; he is concerned to reveal and rescue the individual.

But there is another sense in which society may be said to corrupt. With the best will in the world, we can hardly help being misled by generalizations. And this would apply, more or less, in any society. But existing society (the society of the eighteenth century) went out of its way to conceal men from one another. Between large sections of them, at any rate, there could be no question of understanding, because society sometimes forbade, and always discouraged, com-

[1] R. H. Tawney, *Religion and the Rise of Capitalism* (London, 1926), p. 184.

plete frankness and sincerity. In this respect Mandeville agrees with Clifford about the disadvantages of wealth:

> Such is the condition of the rich. They can scarcely ever know the real inward workings of the people about them. They live in the midst of a stage play, where every one that approaches them is a personated actor, and the lord himself is the only real character, performing his part in good earnest, while the rest are employed in a mummery, and laugh in their hearts at the gross delusion they are practising upon him.[1]

But this, of course, is not true only of the rich. In this passage Godwin is speaking chiefly of flattery; but flattery is not the only way in which men are deceived. In every class a man is compelled to keep his end up, to show a bold face to the world, to conceal many of his true feelings. It is worth noticing that there is a single theme in all Godwin's novels: the tragedy of loneliness and misunderstanding. Each of his heroes is cut off from his fellow men: Caleb Williams by the machinations of Falkland; Mandeville by his riches, his upbringing, his prejudices; St. Leon by the unlucky accident of finding the secret of wealth and immortality; Fleetwood, 'the new man of feeling', by his own romanticism and the consequent disillusion and cynicism which makes him incapable of friendship.

It will be clear that this was something of an obsession with Godwin; and there were, of course, personal reasons for it. There can be no doubt that Godwin suffered a good deal from the torrent of abuse directed against him: he did feel, during a great part of his life, cut off from the great bulk of his fellows and misunderstood by them. He has been represented as a monster of coldness, incapable of any warmth of feeling or of common affection;[2] but his letters belie this. A cold man

[1] *Mandeville*, iii. 91–92.
[2] See, for example, Alexander Gray's *The Socialist Tradition* (London, 1946), p. 115.

does not indulge in violent quarrels with his friends followed by mawkish reconciliations. Godwin did this constantly. He had an almost morbid craving for friendship, hampered by a stiff and pedantic manner, an exceptional touchiness, and a comparative lack of humour. In spite of his friendship with Holcroft, Lamb, Shelley, Coleridge, and all the rest, Godwin was, I imagine, thinking of himself when he made Fleetwood say: 'A friend (a friend, in perhaps the romantic sense of the word) I have never had.'[1]

St. Leon goes farther:

Friendship is a necessity of our nature, the stimulating and restless want of every susceptible heart. How wretched an imposture in this point of view does human life for the most part appear! With boyish eyes, full of sanguine spirits and hope, we look round us for a friend; we sink into the grave, broken down with years and infirmities, and still have not the object of our search. We talk to one man, and he does not understand us; we address ourselves to another, and we find him the unreal similitude only of what we believed him to be. We ally ourselves to a man of intellect and worth; upon further experience we cannot deny him either of these qualities; but the more we know each other, the less we find of resemblance; he is cold, where we are warm; he is harsh, where we are melted into the tenderest sympathy; what fills us with rapture is regarded by him with indifference; we finish with a distant respect, where we looked for a commingling soul; this is not friendship.[2]

There is more than a merely personal obsession here. Godwin believed that society creates misunderstanding, because it fosters certain attitudes that make men incapable of seeing things (and people) as they are. In this, as in most else, he has been misinterpreted. Leslie Stephen could[3] not understand why Godwin thought that *Caleb Williams* illustrated

---

[1] *Fleetwood* (London, 1805), ii. 173.   [2] *St. Leon*, iv. 253.
[3] *Studies of a Biographer* (London, 1902), iii. 145.

his social theories. The hero's sufferings, he pointed out, were not due to the government at all, but to Falkland. This is a startling example of the occasional obtuseness of clever men. What Godwin meant, of course, was that Caleb Williams's sufferings were the direct result of attitudes engendered by society—Falkland's own attitudes in the first place, and secondly those he was able to take advantage of. Godwin, in fact, meant very much what the modern social anthropologist means when he talks of culture patterns.

It is true that Godwin speaks, not of attitudes engendered by society, but of government. It is government that 'insinuates itself into our personal dispositions and insensibly communicates its own spirit to our private transactions'.[1] But this is because Godwin was influenced here by Montesquieu, and Montesquieu regards the form of government as the key institution which enables us to understand the whole culture pattern. In the same way some modern anthropologists regard the family as the key institution. They would say that the way in which children are brought up determines the 'basic personality structure' in a given culture, and explains most of the characteristic features of the culture. For Marxists, on the other hand, economic institutions play this role. But in the eighteenth century the current 'explanation' of society was in terms of political institutions; and this is largely because of Montesquieu.

In his diary for 1791 Godwin says of *Political Justice*: 'My original conception proceeded on a feeling of the imperfections and errors of Montesquieu, and a desire of supplying a less faulty work.'[2] Brailsford, who quotes this and calls attention to its importance, seems to think that Godwin meant Montesquieu's theories about climate. But actually the effect of climate on political institutions is only a small part of Montesquieu's theory of society. At the time Godwin

[1] *P.J.* i. 4.   [2] Quoted in C. Kegan Paul, *William Godwin*, i. 67.

wrote Montesquieu was fashionable. In the year 1790, to give one piece of evidence, a curious little volume was published by the Reverend John Adams, the title-page of which is worth quoting in full. Here it is:

Curious Thoughts on the History of Man; chiefly abridged or selected from the celebrated works of Lord Kaimes, Lord Monboddo, Dr. Dunbar, and the immortal Montesquieu: replete with useful and entertaining instruction, on a variety of important and popular subjects; viz., Population, Language, Manners, Property, Love, Matrimony, Polygamy, Marriage-ceremonies, Commerce, Government, Patriotism, Agriculture, Peace and War, Taxes, Music, Gaming, Luxury, etc.; designed to promote a spirit of enquiry in the youth of both sexes, and to make the philosophy, as well as history of the human species, familiar to ordinary capacities.

It will be seen that Montesquieu gets special emphasis, amounting to what would be called in the theatre 'preferential billing'; and this is made even more obvious by the type and layout of the original. It will be seen also that this is a popular digest meant for the young; and it may be inferred that the social theories of these writers, and of Montesquieu in particular, were becoming part of the contemporary climate of opinion. That such a volume could be published in 1790 does help to explain why Godwin should, in 1791, have made the diary entry quoted above. He was dissatisfied with what was fast becoming, in some circles at least, a received opinion. And it is noteworthy that there is very little in this volume about the effects of climate on character; and that little rather deprecatory than otherwise.

What chiefly impressed Godwin's contemporaries, including the Reverend John Adams, was Montesquieu's classification of governments into three main types, with a corresponding 'spirit' for each. The 'spirit' of a government is not at all unlike the twentieth-century concept of the 'basic personality structure' in a culture. Any government, the argument runs, will quite inevitably encourage certain attitudes of mind among its subjects, and discourage others. As a corollary, it will also find itself encouraging or discouraging certain kinds of institution. The attitudes, and the institutions, will differ according to the type of government. The patterns thus established are so closely knit that Montesquieu felt he could use a single word to describe the spirit of each type of government. The spirit of a despotism is fear; in a monarchy it is honour; in a republic it is virtue.

We need not spend much time on the first of these; and, indeed, Montesquieu himself did not. He was content to say that in a despotic State everything depends on the arbitrary fiat of the despot. This unlimited power descends to subordinate officials, except that each is answerable with his head to the official above him. 'Le vizir est le despote lui-même, et chaque officier particulier est le vizir.'[1] Otherwise a constitution would be necessary; and with the reign of law a despotism is transformed into a monarchy. In this situation nothing is demanded of the citizen except blind obedience. Education is reduced to a minimum, since no one wants the subject to think for himself. 'Il faut . . . faire un mauvais sujet, pour faire un bon esclave.'[2]

The chief interest is in the contrast between republic and monarchy. Throughout L'Esprit des Lois there is a curious mixture of description and prescription; and the prescription is, as it were, at two levels. At times he seems to be saying, with complete scientific impartiality: Monarchies are like this, republics are like that. But the more the scientist generalizes the less is he completely descriptive. It becomes apparent that Montesquieu is not so much describing actual republics or monarchies as laying down the ideal type of

---

[1] Montesquieu, Œuvres complètes . . . (Paris, 1816), i. 120 (bk. v, ch. 19). All references are to this edition.　　[2] Op. cit. i. 60 (iii, 4).

republic or monarchy. The type is 'ideal', it is true, only in the sense of being truly the type; it is, as we say, the perfect specimen, where 'perfect' is not primarily a value word. But value terms inevitably creep in here. Thus we find Montesquieu saying that it is not that one will necessarily have virtue in a republic, or honour in a monarchy, or fear in a despotism, but that one ought to; otherwise the government will be imperfect.[1] 'Imperfect' here possibly means 'not a perfect specimen'; but there is more than a hint of the normal meaning.

But at least, it might be said, Montesquieu is not concerned to ask which is the better form of government. Actually, however, there is little doubt about his preferences. (There is even less doubt about those of the Reverend Mr. Adams. Nothing could be further from the anthropologist's attitude than his citing, as proof of 'the depression of mind in the subjects of despotism', the failure of the Romans to find the funeral rites of the Emperors ridiculous!) Montesquieu himself denounces despotism throughout, as might have been expected. What is perhaps more surprising is his comparative lukewarmness about republics.

In the seventeenth and eighteenth centuries the idea of a republic carried with it all the hallowed associations of classical antiquity. Republicanism was not, indeed, thought of as a practicable political ideal but as the happier dispensation of a remote golden age. The ideal republic was (incomprehensible though this seems to us) Sparta; and the Spartan virtues were a useful stick with which to beat modern selfishness and softness. The denunciation of luxury was a favourite pulpit recreation; and a republic was, briefly, a place where there was no luxury and much public spirit.

The revenues of Geneva [says Adams] scarcely amount to thirty thousand pounds a year; which however, by a well-regulated

<hr />

[1] Op. cit., p. 52.

œconomy, is more than sufficient to defray the current expenses. And this republic is enabled to provide for the security of its subjects, from an income, which many individuals, both in France and England, squander in vain pomp, and vicious dissipation.

A republic, so modelled, inspires virtues of every sort. The people of Switzerland seldom think of writing to confirm a bargain. A lawsuit is scarce known among them; and there are many, who never heard of a counsellor, nor of an attorney. Their doors are never shut but in winter.[1]

There is a good deal of all this in Montesquieu; but on the whole he is inclined to raise his hat to the republic and pass by on the other side. When he says that the spirit, or principle, of a republic is virtue, he is using virtue in a rather special sense. 'Je parle ici de la vertu politique, qui est la vertu morale, dans le sens qu'elle se dirige au bien général; fort peu des vertus morales particulières; et point du tout de cette vertu qui a du rapport aux vérités révélées.'[2] He means, in short, public spirit, or patriotism; public spirit as it was fostered in Sparta.

Why is virtue, in this sense, more necessary in a republic than in a monarchy? There are two main reasons. First, a republic demands restraints on human nature in ways that a monarchy does not. A monarchy depends on the adroit manipulation of common passions, like vanity and ambition. It is essential to a monarchy that there shall be a hierarchy of ranks, or social classes. Honour demands that one shall do what is fitting to one's rank; and this is a sufficient motive to keep the wheels of society turning. In a well-regulated monarchy people behave like good citizens without any real public spirit; they are moved by ambition: '. . . il se trouve que chacun va au bien commun, croyant aller à ses intérêts particuliers'.[3]

---

[1] *Curious Thoughts on the History of Man* (Dublin, 1790), p. 173.
[2] Montesquieu, op. cit. i. 42. [3] Ibid., p. 46 (bk. iii).

In a republic, on the other hand, personal ambition must be repressed. Ambition must be limited to one desire, to do more for one's country than others do. Since a republic demands equality of wealth and simplicity in living, there is no room for avarice. The good citizen of the republic wants only necessaries for himself and his family; superfluities are reserved for his country. Consequently, sumptuary laws will be necessary in a republic; and the size of estates will be kept down by law. Montesquieu does, it is true, qualify this rather curiously. If the republic is commercial rather than agricultural, large fortunes will not matter since commerce brings its own discipline of frugality. 'L'esprit de commerce entraîne avec soi celui de frugalité, d'économie, de modération, de travail, de sagesse, de tranquillité, d'ordre et de règle.'[1] But the spirit of commerce must be maintained by seeing that it reigns alone, and is not mixed with a different spirit, that all the laws favour it, that fortunes are proportionate to commercial success, that the poor have opportunities of taking part in commerce, and that the rich are not tempted to stop working. This is, of course, the *laissez-faire* ideal; and it would seem from this passage that republics may, like monarchies, use passions like avarice rather than suppress them. But this is not Montesquieu's usual view. Generally he represents the republic as requiring extreme selflessness. The single permitted passion is love of country. In monarchies, on the other hand, the social virtues themselves are cunningly linked to love of self. The virtues are less what we owe to others than what we owe to ourselves; they do not so much unite us to our fellow citizens as distinguish us from them. Actions are judged not as *bonnes*, but as *belles*, not as just, but as great, not as reasonable, but as extraordinary.

Secondly, public spirit is less necessary in a monarchy because it depends, far more than a republic, on the reign of

[1] Montesquieu, op. cit., p. 85 (bk. v).

law. A monarchy differs from a despotic state in that the powers of the sovereign are limited by the constitution. But this means that the rights of all ranks in society will tend to be specified by law. Moreover, since there are distinctions of rank, different types of property, and so on, the laws will be complex, and the formalities of justice will be elaborated. It is also quite natural in a monarchy, with its social distinctions, that there should be judges specially skilled in interpreting the law. In a republic, on the other hand, the sentiment will be: let the people judge! But this tends to reduce all legal questions to very simple questions of fact. The subtleties of law are lost in a republic; and it is on these, Montesquieu notes, that the liberty of the subject really depends.

Further, it is necessary in a republic to regulate, not merely public actions, but sentiments and private lives—in a word, the *mœurs* of the citizen. So much depends on public spirit that everything must be done to see that no one backslides. And backsliding may begin in all kinds of indirect ways. Women must be chaste, for example, since the loss of chastity brings so many vices in its train. Among the Romans adultery was a public crime, since the State could not but be interested in 'une si grande violation des mœurs'. Good legislators, Montesquieu adds, proscribe in their republics not only vice but the appearance of vice, so that women must be modest, and not merely chaste. In monarchies, on the other hand, women have little modesty, since 'chacun se sert de leurs agréments et leurs passions pour avancer sa fortune'.[1] Moreover, vanity in women takes the place of pride of achievement in men.

The *censor morum*, then, is an appropriate institution in a republic, but not in a monarchy. So is the common informer, since each citizen is expected to feel unlimited zeal for the

[1] Montesquieu, op. cit., p. 193 (bk. vii).

State, and to have all the rights of the State in his own person. But in a monarchy accusation is best left to a public official, since the informer may have his eye on the riches of the accused.

There is indeed no part of a citizen's life that may not interest the State in a republic. Thus Montesquieu speaks of 'la belle coutume des Samnites' of appraising their young men for such qualities as public spirit, and then allowing them to choose from the young women strictly in order of merit, so that the most deserving had first choice, and so on.

'L'amour, la beauté, la chasteté, la vertu, la naissance, les richesses même, tout cela était, pour ainsi dire, le dot de la vertu. Il seroit difficile d'imaginer une récompense plus noble, plus grande, moins à charge à un petit état, plus capable d'agir sur l'un et l'autre sexe.'[1]

Montesquieu speaks here, it will be noticed, with approval; and I am not suggesting that in general he condemns the republican ideal. Very often he seems to echo the conventional praises of classical patriotism and frugality. I think myself that his tone is rather warmer when he speaks of monarchy; but, however that may be, and whether Montesquieu himself was critical or not, it is not hard to extract from his account of the republic two major lines of criticism.

One is that the republican ideal, though no doubt very noble, does rather too much violence to human nature. The other is that it is, on the whole, prejudicial to the liberty of the individual. This is of course the burden of most modern criticism of socialism; the germs of it are certainly present in Montesquieu.

Against the republican ideal of 'virtue' is set the monarchic one of honour. This is of course what we are inclined to think of as the aristocratic ideal; though Montesquieu uses the term 'aristocracy' in a different sense, to refer to a republic

[1] Montesquieu, op. cit. i. 305 (bk. vii).

where the citizen body is restricted to a section of the total population. But it is of the essence of a monarchy that there should be different ranks and orders of society, and that each citizen should have a lively sense of what is due to his rank. It is 'against the spirit of a monarchy' that the nobility should engage in commerce; this, he says, is one of the things that has weakened monarchy in England. It is also 'against the spirit of commerce', since the nobility will have an unfair advantage, and are likely to acquire monopolies. 'Le commerce est la profession des gens égaux.'[1] The kind of commercial society in which inequalities of wealth and so of status are combined with equality of opportunity is, as we have seen, regarded by Montesquieu as a republic; though he does not seem to have considered the modifications of the republican 'spirit' that would occur in such a State.

A monarchy, then, is for Montesquieu essentially an aristocratic society, and its 'principle', or 'spirit', is the aristocratic ideal of honour. 'L'HONNEUR, c'est à dire le préjugé de chaque personne et de chaque condition, prend la place de la vertu politique dont j'ai parlé, et la représente partout. Il y peut inspirer les plus belles actions; il peut, joint à la force des lois, conduire au but du gouvernement comme la vertu même.'[2]

There are, Montesquieu says, three chief rules of honour: (1) you may take steps to save your fortune, but not your life; (2) you must do nothing and suffer nothing unbecoming to your station in society; (3) unwritten laws are the most binding. As we have seen, honour exacts virtuous behaviour as something due to oneself, rather than to others—truthfulness, for example, comes not from love of truth, but from the desire to seem bold and free, and careless of the opinion of others; politeness from pride rather than from a genuine desire to please. Honour may, however, permit trickery when

[1] Montesquieu, op. cit. i. 96 (bk. v).   [2] Ibid., i. 44 (bk. iii).

associated with grand designs, or infidelity when associated with grand passions.

We shall proceed, in the next two chapters, to Godwin's criticism of Montesquieu. At the moment I want to show how much he was influenced by him (whether directly or indirectly through Rousseau and the general climate of opinion). We shall not otherwise understand what Godwin meant by perfectibility.

The notion of human perfectibility has been much ridiculed from Godwin's day to ours. Godwin himself points out that he did not mean that human beings were perfect or would ever be perfect, but rather that they would always be imperfect. That is to say, there would always be room for improvement.

Human beings, he believed, were infinitely malleable. Hume, who recognized, more than most of his predecessors, the extent to which men were moulded by society, thought nevertheless that some features of human nature were quite unalterable. It just was a psychological law that men would always prefer the nearer interest, once it had become very near, to the more remote. On Monday we are capable of seeing that Tuesday's debauch is not worth Wednesday's headache; but we can no longer see this on Tuesday. It will always be necessary, then, to have rulers whose immediate interest is the remoter interest of their subjects. They can tip the scales in favour of sobriety by seeing to it that Tuesday's excesses have unpleasant consequences on Tuesday as well as on Wednesday. This is almost the whole art of government.

All that Godwin is saying is that it is at least doubtful whether we can say, quite so definitely, at what point human nature stops and the influence of society begins. It is quite obvious from Montesquieu's account that the citizen of a republic is a very different creature from the citizen of a monarchy. He is different because his attitudes and values are different: or, as Godwin would put it, his opinions.

The controversy has been renewed in our own day, by the social psychologists and the anthropologists. And the prevailing opinion is now on Godwin's side. It is now suggested that even the temperamental differences between the sexes may be the result of cultural rather than physical causes. This is precisely the kind of assertion that Godwin made. I am not suggesting that this theory has been 'proved' by 'science'; the fashionable opinion of the moment may or may not be right. All that I want to say is that Godwin was no more visionary nor obviously absurd than Margaret Mead or Bronislaw Malinowski.[1]

The modern anthropologist is not concerned to draw the conclusion that, if you want to change human nature, you can do it by remodelling society. Godwin was. But he did not think that the change could be made simply, overnight, by a revolution or even by a few well-chosen syllogisms. When Godwin rebukes the ardent young Shelley, he does so quite in the spirit of the modern anthropologist, almost in the spirit of Burke:

One principle that I believe is wanting in you, and in all our too fervent and impetuous reformers, is the thought that almost every institution and form of society is good in its place and in the period

[1] For a grandiloquent illustration of the general theory, see Godwin's *Life of Chaucer*, 1803, ii. 317: 'All nature must be set in motion to make a poet. Every thing within the circumference of political society must concur to ripen his talents and expand his powers, to feed his reflections with wholesome aliment, and to awaken in him the consciousness of what he is. Nothing can more strongly confirm this theory than the example of Chaucer. When did England first produce a man, since the revival of literature, worthy to be called a poet? When the enormous and cumbersome mass of the feudal system was more than half crumbled away, when the popular part of our constitution began to rear its head, and man in a collective sense learned to look inward upon himself.' See also Godwin's preface, p. viii.

of time to which it belongs. . . . There is a period, indeed, when each institution is obsolete, and should be laid aside; but it is of much importance that we should not proceed too rapidly in this, or introduce any change before its due and proper season. . . .[1]

And this was, for Godwin, no new discovery.

There are few truths more striking in the history of human affairs [he had proclaimed in his *Life of Chaucer*] than that things which may be hurtful and injurious in one stage of society, had probably their period in a different stage when they were eminently advantageous and salutary. No speculation can do less credit to the discernment of its authors, than that which, examining institutions and practices in the abstract, decides indiscriminately that this is good and universally desirable, while that is fitted only to be the plague of mankind. Every thing has its place.[2]

There is indeed a problem here. If Godwin believed that opinions resulted from the structure of society, why did he advocate trying to change opinion rather than society? The answer is that he fully realized the dilemma involved in the whole question whether one should first change men's hearts or their institutions. It appears that you cannot change either without first changing the other. Godwin did not conclude that the problem was therefore insoluble; but he did realize that any sudden or easy change was impossible.

The problem may be put in another way: Value judgements ('opinions about what is desirable') depend on social institutions; but you cannot change social institutions unless men think the change desirable. (It is not enough to impose the change by force, because the new social institutions will not work unless men already have the appropriate attitudes.) The problem may seem to be insoluble. And so indeed it would be, if attitudes were appropriate only to the social institutions that engender them. But there is, for Godwin,

[1] Godwin to Shelley, 4 Mar. 1812. Quoted in C. Kegan Paul, *William Godwin*, ii. 205–6.   [2] See i, p. 161. See also i. 125.

another sense in which they can be called appropriate. There are some attitudes that will result quite automatically from seeing things as they are. In one way, this only poses the problem in another form; for institutions may be favourable or unfavourable to seeing things as they are. But men cannot be totally blind to all the facts for ever. If institutions are not favourable, then there will at least be some point at which there is some chance of changing them so as to make them a little more favourable; and this opens the way to further changes; and so on. We must not expect reason to take men's hearts by storm; we must settle down to a long, slow siege. Or, as Godwin wrote to Shelley: 'He that would benefit mankind on a comprehensive scale, by changing the principles and elements of society, must learn the hard lesson, to put off self, and to contribute by a quiet but incessant activity, like a rill of water, to irrigate and fertilise the intellectual evil.'[1]

Godwin does not, then, in what he says about perfectibility, make any very extravagant claims. All he is really insisting on is that we should not rule out the possibility of a change in human behaviour; that we should not take the patterns of our own time and country as the fixed and unalterable human pattern.

The point comes out clearly in his controversy with Malthus. The celebrated *Essay on Population* was inspired by Godwin.[2] There was nothing new in the general thesis that any attempt to raise the standing of living of the poor would be self-stultifying, since the poor, when fed, would merely breed more rapidly. In *Political Justice* Godwin thought it necessary to meet the objection in the form in which it had

[1] Godwin to Shelley, 14 Mar. 1812. Quoted in C. Kegan Paul, *William Godwin*, ii. 207.

[2] In his introduction Malthus refers to Godwin's essay *On Avarice and Profusion* in *The Enquirer*, but in the *Essay on Population* itself he pays much more attention to the arguments in *Political Justice*, bk. viii, ch 9.

been put by Robert Wallace; and the *Essay on Population* is really Malthus's reply to Godwin's reply to Wallace. Godwin replied to Malthus in *Thoughts on Dr. Parr's Spital Sermon* and in *Of Population*.

I shall take Bonar's account of the controversy, because it brings out clearly the usual misunderstanding of Godwin. According to Bonar, Godwin makes two main points. First, he points out that 'three fourths of the habitable globe are now uncultivated': it would take 'myriads of centuries' to break in all the virgin land and fill it with people. Secondly, he argues that human nature may change in the meantime; men may learn to control the urge to reproduce. Bonar dismisses the first point as irrelevant, the second as Utopian. Wallace and Malthus are stating a universal law of nature which operates all the time, and 'ought not to be stated in terms of time at all'. 'Where goods increase, they are increased that eat them.' As for the second point, Malthus is entitled to reply:

If you told me that man was becoming a winged creature like the ostrich, I should not doubt that he would find wings very useful, but I could hardly believe your prophecy without some kind of proof beyond the mere praises of flying. I should ask you to show some palpable signs in his body and neck that such a change was going on, that his neck has been lengthening, his lips hardening, his hair becoming feathery. In the same way, when you tell me that man is becoming a purely intellectual being, content with plain living and high thinking, I see there might be advantage in the change, but I ask for signs that it is in progress. I see none; but, on the contrary, I see strong reasons for believing in its impossibility.[1]

Most of this is a complete misapprehension of Godwin. He does not mean that progress is inevitable, so that only provided we allow for a sufficient lapse of time, men will

[1] James Bonar, *Malthus and His Work* (2nd ed., London, 1924), ch. 1.

behave like angels. All he says is that it is unsafe to suppose that sociological 'laws', drawn from the behaviour of human beings in a particular social setting, will continue to apply in the remote future. It is, indeed, Godwin who is accusing Malthus of being 'abstract'. In *Thoughts on Man* he makes the point explicitly:

Arithmetic, unsubjected to the impulses of passion and the accidents of created nature, holds on its course; but, in the phenomena of the actual world, 'time and chance happeneth to them all'. Thus it is, for example, in the arithmetical and geometrical ratios, set up in political economy by the celebrated Mr. Malthus. His numbers will go on smoothly enough, 1, 2, 4, 8, 16, 32, as representing the principle of population among mankind, and 1, 2, 3, 4, 5, 6, the means of subsistence; but restiff and uncomplying nature refuses to conform herself to his dicta.[1]

It is perhaps only fair to add that Godwin gives an unfortunate example:

Morse, in his American Gazetteer, proceeding on the principles of Malthus, tells us that, if the city of New York goes on increasing for a century in a certain ratio, it will by that time contain 5,257,493 inhabitants. But does anyone, for himself or his posterity, expect to see this reached?

Actually, however, the growth of New York was not due to natural increase. And on the question at issue Godwin has surely been vindicated. No doubt the worker at the time of the industrial revolution, living in semi-starvation and bestial

---

[1] *Thoughts on Man* (London, 1831), pp. 394–5. Godwin makes this point throughout the book, *Of Population* (London, 1820), which he wrote in reply to Malthus. 'The strength of Mr. Malthus's writing wholly depends upon his intrenching himself in general statements. If we hope for any victory over him, it must be by drawing him out of his stronghold, and meeting him upon the fair ground of realities' (p. 27). And again: ' . . . the misery of all our author's reasonings upon human affairs is, that they are pictureless, and dwell entirely in abstractions and generalities' (p. 572).

conditions, took no thought for the morrow, and clutched at the pleasure of the moment. Call this human nature if you like. But the fact remains that his descendants, in New Zealand perhaps or the U.S.A., given a standard of living that Malthus would have thought Utopian, are now accused, by the spiritual descendants of Malthus, of 'putting the baby car before the baby', of being too selfish to have children. It is not necessary to suppose that human beings are 'becoming purely intellectual beings' to believe that they will behave very differently in different social settings.

It is interesting to notice that Malthus misinterprets Godwin in much the same way as Leslie Stephen. 'And certain it is', he writes in a private letter, 'that almost under the worst form of government, where there was any tolerable freedom of competition, the race of labourers, by not marrying, and consequently decreasing their numbers, might immediately better their condition, and under the very best form of government, by marrying and greatly increasing their numbers, they would immediately make their condition worse.'[1] Godwin's point is, of course, that whether or not they will in fact marry depends on attitudes engendered by the social pattern or, on his (and Montesquieu's) analysis, on the form of government. He might have quoted Montesquieu himself in his support:

'Les femelles des animaux ont à peu près une fécondité constante. Mais, dans l'espèce humaine, la manière de penser, le caractère, les passions, les fantaisies, les caprices, l'idée de conserver sa beauté, l'embarras de la grossesse, celui d'une famille trop nombreuse, troublent la propagation de mille manières.'[1]

It is precisely this kind of attitude that varies in different

---

[1] Malthus to Godwin, 20 Aug. 1798. Quoted in C. Kegan Paul, *William Godwin*, i. 324.

[2] *Esprit des Lois*, bk. xxiii, ch. i, vol. ii, p. 362.

cultures.[1] In taking account of them it is Godwin who is the realist and Malthus who is the abstract theorist. All that the doctrine of human perfectibility means is that we should not lose sight of such factors. We should not regard the contemporary form of society as immutable and God-given, or the men it produces as somehow eternally Man.

[1] 'Mr. Malthus says: "the passion between the sexes is necessary, and will always remain nearly in its present state". . . . I would ask, what is its present state? The want of a precise explanation under this head is a deficiency that goes to the heart of the system. Mr. Malthus assumes something that is perpetually shifting, that at no two periods, and in no two places, is alike, and treats it as if it were absolutely determinate. . . . This . . . proposition, if explicitly unfolded, must mean that 'the passion between the sexes' always exists and acts, in all persons, in all countries, and in all ages of the world, under all institutions, prejudices, superstitions, and systems of thinking, in the same manner. But when the whole meaning that lies hid in this ambiguous proposition has been thus unfolded, I suppose it will not find a single defender.' *Of Population* (London, 1820), p. 530.

4

THE INSUFFICIENCY OF HONOUR

WE can now see what puzzled Leslie Stephen, and can see how *Caleb Williams* illustrates Godwin's social theories. *Caleb Williams* is written primarily as a 'series of adventures of flight and pursuit',[1] that is to say, a thriller; but Godwin could no more keep his political opinions out of it than, say, Sapper or John Buchan or Nicholas Blake could keep their political opinions out of their thrillers. Indeed, the comparison reminds us at once that Godwin never regarded his novels as *merely* light entertainment. He was rather depressed than otherwise when Joseph Gerrald told him that, starting *Caleb Williams* late one evening, he could not go to bed until he had finished all three volumes.

Thus, what had cost me twelve months' labour, ceaseless heartaches and industry, now sinking in despair, now roused and sustained in unusual energy, he went over in a few hours, shut the book, laid himself on his pillow, slept and was refreshed, and cried,
'Tomorrow to fresh woods and pastures new'.[2]

In the same preface he tells us, with some apologies, of a 'vainglorious impulse' which, he says, he had kept quiet about for forty years. 'I said to myself a thousand times, "I will write a tale that shall constitute an epoch in the mind of the reader, that no one, after he has read it, shall ever be exactly the same man as he was before!"'[3] And in the preface to the first edition he had said:

What is now presented to the public is no refined and abstract speculation; it is a study and delineation of things passing in the

[1] Preface to 1832 ed. of *Caleb Williams*, Routledge, 1903, p. xix.
[2] Ibid., pp. xxv–xxvi.   [3] Ibid., p. xxi.

moral world. It is but of late that the inestimable importance of political principles has been adequately apprehended. It is now known to philosophers that the spirit and character of the government intrudes itself into every rank of society. But this is a truth highly worthy to be communicated to persons whom books of philosophy and science are never likely to reach. Accordingly it was proposed, in the invention of the following work, to comprehend, as far as the progressive nature of a single story would allow, a general review of the modes of domestic and unrecorded despotism, by which man becomes the destroyer of man.

I have quoted these passages at length in order to show that Godwin's novels may be fairly cited as evidence of his social theory. Indeed they show, more clearly than his avowedly political writing, exactly how he thought of his principles as working out in practice. Nor is it adequate to say, as Mr. Woodcock does, that Godwin's invariable theme is the individual at odds with society. We have already seen that this is, in a sense, true: Godwin does always write of loneliness and misunderstanding, of the individual cut off from his fellows. But his theme is not simply the cruelty of organized society to the suffering underdog. Godwin is not an eighteenth-century Upton Sinclair, or even a Dickens. His characters are nearly always the authors of their own misfortunes. They are cut off by their own prejudices, by their failure to see things as they are. This is certainly less true of *Caleb Williams* than of the later novels; but even here Godwin is being a good deal more subtle than Leslie Stephen (for instance) realized.

His main intention, according to the preface, is to show that 'the spirit and character of government intrudes itself into every rank of society'. This is the contention of the first chapter of *Political Justice*. That Godwin also thought of it as the main theme of the whole book is confirmed by his statement that *Caleb Williams* was 'the offspring of that temper of mind in which the composition of *Political Justice* left me'.[1] Godwin, then, was accepting Montesquieu's thesis that the citizens of a monarchy, like Britain, will quite unconsciously imbibe the characteristic attitudes and ideals that constitute the 'spirit' of a monarchy.

So much was common to Godwin and Montesquieu; and it will be noticed that Godwin regards this as something 'now known to philosophers'—that is to say, as the accepted opinion among those who thought seriously on such topics. It was a 'new, true and important' discovery that needed popularizing. The story of Caleb Williams was to illustrate this principle, by showing how it applied in a concrete situation. To do this it was obviously not necessary to demonstrate, as Leslie Stephen imagined, that Caleb was persecuted by the Government of the day. In fact, he was persecuted by a private enemy, Falkland. But the point is not, as Woodcock seems to think, that Falkland was enabled to persecute Williams because of his position in society, or even that he was able to persecute him by taking advantage of the common social attitudes. That is no doubt part of Godwin's meaning. In the eighteenth century a rich landowner, like Falkland, did have great power over a penniless dependent of no family, like Caleb Williams. No doubt Godwin meant to bring this out. But he also meant to show that Falkland was himself a victim of society quite as much as Williams. Godwin meant, in short, to go beyond Montesquieu by showing that the ideal of Honour was a complete failure. It was a double failure: it did not succeed in creating harmonious social relations so as to make a just and stable society; and it did not make for the inner harmony of those who were permeated by the ideal.

Falkland is a kind of incarnation of the whole ideal of Honour. He is the spirit of Monarchy made visible. In his

[1] Quoted by C. Kegan Paul from Godwin's diary. C. Kegan Paul, *William Godwin*, i. 78.

1832 preface Godwin tells us how he conceived Falkland. His account fits in well enough with my interpretation, even though he is referring only to the dramatic needs of the story and not to its social significance.

Nor could my purpose of giving an overpowering interest to my tale be answered, without his appearing to have been originally endowed with a mighty store of amiable dispositions and virtues, so that his being driven to the first act of murder should be judged worthy of the deepest regret, and should be seen in some measure to have arisen out of his virtues themselves. It was necessary to make him, so to speak, the tenant of an atmosphere of romance, so that every reader should feel prompted almost to worship him for his high qualities.[1]

We are told, accordingly, that Falkland had been influenced in his childhood by poems of chivalry and romance.

He had too much good sense to regret the times of Charlemagne and Arthur. But . . . he conceived that there was in the manners depicted by these celebrated poets something to imitate, as well as something to avoid. He believed that nothing was so well calculated to make men delicate, gallant and humane, as a temper perpetually alive to the sentiments of birth and honour.[2]

The adjectives 'delicate, gallant and humane' are worth stressing. The man of honour, as Godwin conceived him, is no swashbuckler. Falkland even avoids fighting a duel when he is convinced that it would be senseless and unnecessary. His behaviour to others, and especially his dependants, is not only courteous but genuinely considerate. He is no Philistine either. Falkland is a scholar and a wit; and his neighbours in the country entertain themselves, at fashionable gatherings, by reading his poems aloud. Falkland is indeed not only the Man of Honour, but another eighteenth-century abstraction, the Man of Taste.

[1] Op. cit., p. xx. [2] Op. cit., p. 11.

He is expressly contrasted with a neighbouring squire, Barnabas Tyrrel. If Falkland represents the spirit of Monarchy, Tyrrel is the spirit of Despotism. He is the typical hunting, shooting, drinking squire, hardly capable of any pleasures more refined than those of the palate. He is anxious to be popular, and constitutes himself a village despot, granting and withholding favours to his toadies. He is 'insupportably arrogant, tyrannical to his neighbours, and insolent to his equals'. His temper is capricious: 'When his subjects, encouraged by his familiarity, had discarded their precaution, the wayward fit would seize him, a sudden cloud overspread his brow, his voice transform from the pleasant to the terrible, and a quarrel of a straw immediately ensue with the first man whose face he did not like.'[1] This is precisely the behaviour of Montesquieu's despot; and Godwin makes the parallel more obvious by calling Tyrrel 'a village bashaw'. When Falkland arrives in the neighbourhood, Tyrrel loses his following; and Godwin describes this in terms which suggest the transition from an absolute monarchy to a constitutional one:

The advantages Mr. Falkland possessed in this comparison are palpable; and had it been otherwise, the subjects of his rural neighbour were sufficiently disposed to revolt against his merciless dominion. They had hitherto submitted from fear, not from love; and, if they had not rebelled, it was only for want of a leader.[2]

The advantages of Mr. Falkland are indeed so palpable that the reader may wonder what is wrong, after all, with the ideal of Honour, since it produces such a paragon. To answer this we need, I think, to consider more fully what I have already said about Falkland being also the Man of Taste. We are here concerned with what Godwin had learned, not from Montesquieu, but from Hartley.

[1] Op. cit., p. 22. [2] Op. cit., p. 24.

There is a passage in *Political Justice*[1] in which Godwin constructs what he calls a 'scale of happiness' in four stages. This is fairly obviously a simplified version of Hartley's hierarchy of pleasures.

We may first of all conceive, says Godwin, of an exceptionally uncultivated peasant or artisan, gaining a bare subsistence by hard manual labour, and conscious of very little but the sensation of the moment. 'This man is in a certain sense happy. He is happier than a stone.' But 'the general train of his sensations comes as near as the nature of human existence will admit to the region of indifference'.

As a first refinement on this, we have the man of wealth and fashion, who

enjoys all the luxuries of the palate, the choicest viands, and the best-flavoured wines. He takes his pleasures discreetly, so as not, in the pursuit of pleasure, to lose the power of feeling it. He shoots, he hunts. He frequents all public places. . . . With a happy flow of spirits and a perpetual variety of amusements he is almost a stranger to ennui. But he is a model of ignorance. He never reads, and knows nothing beyond the topic of the day. He can scarcely conceive the meaning of the sublime or pathetic; and he rarely thinks of anything beyond himself. This man is happier than the peasant. He is happier, by all the pleasures of the palate, and all the gratifications of neatness, elegance and splendour, in himself, and the objects around him.

But he is not as happy as he might be. Happier still is the man of taste, who adds to 'the gratifications of expense' an appreciation of the beauties of nature, and of art, and of the pleasures of study.

He admires the overhanging cliff, the wide-extended prospect, the vast expanse of the ocean, the foliage of the woods, the sloping lawn and the waving grass. He knows the pleasures of solitude, when man holds commerce alone with the tranquil solemnity of

[1] *P.J.* i. 444–8.

nature. He has traced the structure of the universe; the substances which compose the globe we inhabit, and are the materials of human industry; and the laws which hold the planets in their course amidst the trackless fields of space. He studies; and has experienced the pleasures which result from conscious perspicacity and discovered truth. He enters, with a true relish, into the sublime and the pathetic. He partakes in all the grandeur and enthusiasm of poetry.

'In this person,' Godwin concludes, 'compared with the two preceding classes, we acknowledge something of the features of men. They were only a better sort of brutes; but he has sensations and transports of which they have no conception.' But something is still lacking. The pleasures of taste are cold, unless they are given meaning by sympathy for others. The whole man has a heart as well as a head. Mere study and aesthetic enjoyment will seem pointless, unless they are somehow interfused with a desire for human happiness. There seem to be two points here: first, that the intellectual pleasures are not themselves fully satisfying, become mere aimless play, unless we feel that they are somehow important for human happiness in general; and, secondly, that the pleasures of benevolence are greater than these. 'The man who has once performed an act of exalted generosity knows that there is no sensation of corporeal or intellectual taste to be compared with this.' The man of benevolence, then, is at the top of the scale of happiness. And his pleasure is disinterested, in the sense that for him doing good is its own reward. 'He ascends to the highest of human pleasures, the pleasures of disinterestedness. . . . No man so truly promotes his own interest, as he that forgets it. No man reaps so copious a harvest of pleasure, as he who thinks only of the pleasures of other men.'

As a commentary on Hartley, this passage could hardly be bettered. Godwin is concerned here only with the central doctrine, that the higher pleasures take up into themselves those below them, and are, largely for that reason, more pleasant. His four types are intended mainly as illustrations. The peasant is little more than the raw human material; the man of wealth exemplifies the pleasures of sense, as refined by the pleasures of imagination of the lower kinds; the man of taste shows us the pleasures of imagination proper; the man of benevolence the pleasures of sympathy. Godwin says nothing of the pleasures of ambition, self-interest, theopathy, or the moral sense, because these are primarily controlling or integrating sentiments rather than immediate sources of pleasure. In any case, he disagreed with Hartley about theopathy and about 'rational self-interest' as another name for hope of heaven and fear of hell; and he wished to stress that the pleasures of sympathy are their own greatest reward, simply in themselves; without also showing, as Hartley does, that they are linked with the more obvious kinds of self-interest. The latter argument is actually necessary in order to support the contention that the pleasures of benevolence outweigh any other possible combination of pleasures. But Godwin is emphasizing the point that benevolence is *felt* to be disinterested, in the consciousness of the benevolent man himself: it is not a matter of nicely calculated less or more; he 'rises above the mechanical ideas of barter and exchange'.

That the omission of theopathy is deliberate is, I think, shown by the fact that Godwin goes on, in the rest of the chapter, to discuss 'the creed of optimism', and to insist on the reality of evil.

A sound philosophy will teach us to contemplate this scene without madness. Instructed in its lessons, we shall remember that, though there is much of evil, there is also much of good in the world, much pleasure as well as much pain. . . . But the optimist must be particularly rash, who takes upon him to affirm of all this mass of evil without exception, that it is relatively not evil, and that nothing could have happened otherwise than it has happened, without the total being worse than it is.[1]

Let us now return to *Caleb Williams*. Tyrrel and Falkland can be regarded, not only as representing the spirit of despotism and of monarchy, but also as illustrating the successive steps of the scale of happiness. There is no need to choose between these two interpretations. It is, of course, part of Godwin's case that neither despotism nor monarchy make their citizens as happy as they might be. And it is important to notice that the question is not one of external, but of internal influences. It is not so much that these States oppress their citizens, but that they mould them so as to make them less capable of attaining the full stature of human beings. Monarchy succeeds better than despotism; but it still falls short.

There is a character in the novel, called Grimes, who may be taken as the counterpart of the peasant or artisan whom Godwin assigns to the first rung of the ladder.

This fellow, without an atom of intentional malice, was fitted, by the mere coarseness of his perceptions, for the perpetration of the greatest injuries. He regarded both injury and advantage merely as they related to the gratification of appetite; and considered it an essential of true wisdom to treat with insult the effeminacy of those who suffer themselves to be tormented with ideal misfortunes.[2]

He is, in short, incapable of almost all the pleasures of imagination.

Tyrrel is, I think, to be taken as the man of wealth. The contrast between Tyrrel and Falkland is precisely the contrast that Godwin draws, in the passage I have quoted, between the man of wealth and the man of taste. Falkland

---

[1] *P.J.* i. 457–8.   [2] *Caleb Williams*, bk. i, ch. 7, p. 78.

has all the charm, the wit, the scholarship, the delicacy of perception that Tyrrel lacks; and Tyrrel is scornful of these effeminate accomplishments. But he is also deeply resentful of them, because he feels obscurely that Falkland outshines him, and he can see that his neighbours certainly think so.

Mr. Falkland he described as an animal that was beneath contempt. Diminutive and dwarfish in his form, he wanted to set up a new standard of human nature, adapted to his miserable condition. He wished to persuade people that the human species were made to be nailed to a chair, and to pore over books. He would have them exchange those robust exercises which make us joyous in the performance, and vigorous in the consequences, for the wise labour of scratching our heads for a rhyme and counting our fingers for a verse. Monkeys were as good men as these. A nation of such animals would have no chance with a single regiment of the Old English votaries of beef and pudding. He never saw anything come of learning but to make people foppish and impertinent; and a sensible man would not wish a worse calamity to the enemies of his nation, than to see them run mad after such pernicious absurdities. It was impossible that people could seriously feel any liking for such a ridiculous piece of goods as this outlandish foreign-made Englishman. But he knew very well what it was: it was a miserable piece of mummery that was played only in spite of him. But God for ever blast his soul, if he were not bitterly revenged upon them all![1]

For Tyrrel, then, there is only the sentiment of ambition to organize his impulses. We are told that he has a secret dread of finding himself an outcast. This is no doubt partly because he senses that his insensibility to the higher pleasures is a lack in himself, and one which others despise him for. The fate he fears overtakes him because of this very lack of refinement. Without taste or benevolence he is unable to achieve even his limited aim of popularity and respect. He is driven by his obscure resentment to lengths of persecution

[1] *Caleb Williams*, bk. i, ch. 3, p. 25.

which his neighbours cannot condone even for the sake of his wealth and his coarse generosity. As Hartley might have put it, gross self-interest[1] is not enough, even for the aims which it sets itself.

Falkland is to find that refined self-interest is not enough either. It is not quite accurate to call him merely a man of taste. He is full of the most genuine and perceptive sympathy. But Falkland falls short of true benevolence because with him, as with Tyrrel, the controlling sentiment is still ambition, the desire for respect, though in a much more subtle form. In Falkland, as we have seen, it becomes the aristocratic ideals of honour and chivalry. After he has been overwhelmed by disaster, he refers to himself more than once as 'the fool of honour'. Honour includes pride in taste and artistic ability as well as in manly prowess. Honour demands that he shall be considerate and sympathetic, especially to his social inferiors; but his benevolence is more a kind of good taste than a genuine passion for the happiness of humanity; and it is subordinate, in the last analysis, to the desire for prestige. As a result he is able, when publicly humiliated by Tyrrel, to murder him in a fit of blind passion; to allow an innocent man to be hanged for the murder; and to persecute Caleb Williams, who stumbles upon the secret. Falkland's ambition, like Tyrrel's, is self-stultifying. For, although he retains the respect of his neighbours, he loses the self-respect that is a necessary part of his pride, and he ends his days in melancholy and madness.

A curious comment in the memoir attached to the 1832 edition suggests that Godwin was successful in making Falkland mirror the contemporary ideal, even though the moral was not entirely appreciated. *Caleb Williams*, we are told, was popular because 'all that might have offended as hard and

---

[1] This is not quite accurate, since for Hartley gross self-interest includes the aesthetic pleasures.

republican in his larger work was obliterated [in this smaller one] by the splendour and noble beauty of the character of Falkland'.[1]

Falkland does, indeed, show the aristocratic type in its most favourable form. Contemporary society, Godwin says elsewhere, did much to encourage the more despotic type of character. In *Caleb Williams* we are told that Tyrrel became what he was because his mother spoiled him and because his companions, mostly of an inferior social class, were unable to withstand his whims. In *Political Justice* Godwin suggests that this will be true of all princes, whether absolute or limited in their constitutional powers; and hardly less true of the aristocracy in general. The whole system of class distinction is one great obstacle to seeing men and society as they really are: both Tyrrel and Falkland are, in their different ways, ruined by this. Godwin's other main point is that Montesquieu is quite wrong in supposing that, in a class society, everyone will work for the common good while thinking only of his own interest. In the last resort, as the story of Falkland shows, you can only make people act benevolently by making them benevolent. It is not enough simply to make them proud. It is really surprising that Godwin should have made himself so unpopular through insisting on this, when one considers how unpopular Bernard Mandeville became through asserting the opposite.

Godwin returns to this theme in almost all his novels. Of *Mandeville* he says: 'It is the express purpose of the narrative in which I am engaged, to show how the concurrence of a variety of causes operate to form a character.'[2] The book is actually a study of bigotry; and, in spite of its wordy rhetoric, the reader does get some impression of a man hag-ridden by his own prejudices. After a lonely childhood, without playmates, Mandeville is sent to Winchester. Too

---

[1] Op. cit., p. vi.   [2] *Mandeville* (London, 1817), i. 280.

solitary and reserved to be popular, yet intensely ambitious and anxious for friendship, he becomes very jealous of the popular and accomplished Clifford. This hatred embitters his whole life. He comes to persecute Clifford much as Falkland had persecuted Caleb Williams. As with Falkland, his main motive is a perverted sense of honour. Mandeville is, for example, given to soliloquies of this kind:

That I, descended from one of the first families, and in immediate succession to one of the largest estates in England, should have been addressed with this indignity, was a thought that could never be blotted out from the record of my brain; by day and by night it accompanied me; in solitude and society it haunted me; it mixed with all my dreams and all my reveries; if a moment of festivity or peace came over me unawares, it was presently poisoned by the withering recollection—'I am a blasted branch—the tremendous gale of public disgrace has passed over all the buds of my promise, and I am nothing.'[1]

What is made clearer than in the parallel case of Falkland is that this obsession prevents Mandeville from seeing things as they are. He continually misunderstands Clifford and misinterprets his motives, and this causes the whole tragedy. The moral is quite obvious. A society in which every man is primarily concerned with keeping his end up, jealously watching his own prestige, is not, whatever Montesquieu may think, one in which men will be clear-sighted or will live in harmony.

Another Man of Honour is St. Leon. Most commentators have seized on Godwin's statement in his introduction that he wanted, in *St. Leon*, to make it clear that he did value domestic affection, in spite of the Archbishop's chambermaid. But Woodcock is, I think, quite right when he says that this is only a minor theme in *St. Leon*; though I disagree with his own interpretation. He thinks that Godwin is saying

---

[1] *Mandeville* (London, 1817), i. 299–300.

that 'a man who attains wisdom and wishes to use it for the general good must expect and be willing to forgo the ordinary comforts of life, and the benefits of domestic affection and even friendship in the course of his efforts'.[1] And Godwin is, he suggests, thinking of his own trials. This would be more convincing if St. Leon's efforts for the general good had been more successful; but in fact they made himself and everyone else miserable. The conclusion would seem to be that it is no use trying to use wisdom for the general good; but Godwin would hardly have said that, even in his most despondent moments. I think, then, that Woodcock is wrong in supposing that the philosopher's stone and the elixir of life which St. Leon possesses stand simply for wisdom.

The theme of *St. Leon* is, I believe, put quite clearly in the novel itself by Marguerite, St. Leon's wife:

A generous spirit, Reginald, delights to live upon equal terms with his associates and fellows. He would disdain, when offered to him, decisive and clandestine advantages. Equality is the soul of all real and cordial society. A man of rank indeed does not live upon equal terms with the whole of his species; but his heart also can exult; for he has his equals. How unhappy the wretch, the monster rather let me say, that is without an equal; that looks through the world, and in the world cannot find a brother; that is endowed with attributes which no living being participates with him; and that is therefore cut off for ever from all cordiality and confidence, can never unbend himself, but lives the solitary, joyless tenant of a prison whose materials are rubies and emeralds! How unhappy this wretch; how weak and ignoble the man that voluntarily accepts these laws of existence.[2]

This is, in short, the old theme of the ideal of Honour defeating itself. The search for prestige is self-stultifying.

[1] George Woodcock, *William Godwin* (London, 1946), p. 159.
[2] *St. Leon*, ii. 235. Cf. the *Life of Chaucer*: 'He felt a prouder, or a more inbred, tranquillity at the sight of living beings with whom he could fraternise, than at feeling himself lord . . .', ii. 399.

What one wants is the respect and admiration of one's fellows; it is supposed that wealth and rank will rouse these emotions; but in fact they only cut one off from those less privileged. St. Leon's predicament is only more complete than the man of rank's; the difference is one of degree; for what saves the man of rank, it will be noticed, is that he has equals, not that he has inferiors.

It is made quite clear that St. Leon is led into his troubles by his sentiments of Honour. Contrasting himself with Marguerite, St. Leon says:

All superfluous appendages and show appeared to her as so many obstacles to enjoyment. She derived her happiness from the tone of her own mind, and stood in no need of the gaping admiration and stupid wonder of others to make her feel herself happy. But I retained still the original vice of my mind. The gestures of worship and the voice of applause were necessary to me. I did not suffice to myself.[1]

Ford K. Brown thinks that Godwin is here thinking of himself and Mary Wollstonecraft; but, while Marguerite is no doubt in general a portrait of Mary, St. Leon is speaking here in character, and it is not necessary to suppose that the character was Godwin's. For he goes on:

When we travelled, it was with an attendance little short of princely. When we were at home, every accidental guest was received and entertained with extraordinary pomp, a pomp not directed to add to his accommodation, but that was designed to leave him impressed with astonishment and admiration at the spirit of his host. Often indeed did I feel this ostentation an incumbrance. Often did I languish for the ease and freedom which result from a mediocrity of circumstance. But this I called, doing honour to my ancestors and my country, and vindicating the consideration due to the house of St. Leon.[2]

[1] *St. Leon*, i. 111.   [2] Ibid., 112–13.

This is hardly Godwin himself. But it is Montesquieu's Man of Honour, rather less sympathetically observed. St. Leon at first refuses to accept the philosopher's stone, which is offered to him on condition of absolute secrecy, because he does not want to have a secret from Marguerite. The mysterious stranger overcomes his resistance by attacking him at his weakest point:

Under the usurping and dishonoured name of virtue, you have sunk into a slavery baser than that of the enchantress Alcina. . . . Years have passed over my head in vain, and I have not learned to distinguish a man of honour from a slave. . . . You are degraded from the rank you once held among mankind; your children are destined to live in the inglorious condition of peasants.[1]

A second main theme of *St. Leon* is the futility of indirect attempts at philanthropy. St. Leon is compelled to use devious means and never to be completely frank; hence he is invariably misunderstood and his plans miscarry. He has unlimited resources and none but benevolent intentions; but because people do not understand what he is trying to do, his efforts to help them are futile. 'There was no horrible calumny they did not invent, or give credit to against me. They imputed the basest personal motives for what I had done.'[2]

This is, of course, the favourite Godwin theme of the need for sincerity. In a society like Montesquieu's monarchy, nine-tenths of our energy goes in emulating our neighbours. We are all of us continually keeping our end up, concealing our weaknesses, taking care not to be caught in our shirt-sleeves. A natural human weakness? No doubt, says Godwin; but none the less the result of a particular social organization. It need not be condemned as 'unnatural'; but it is to be condemned for two reasons. First, because it causes unnecessary strain, and is thus the direct cause of much misery; secondly,

---

[1] *St. Leon*, ii. 8, 9, 11.   [2] Ibid. iv. 74.

because it makes it much harder to cultivate 'appropriate attitudes', attitudes, that is to say, that spring from seeing men as they really are. We do not know them as they are, because we all of us wear masks; we do not know their feelings about us, because they disguise them under a cloak of politeness. The effect is only to make us wonder anxiously what they really think of us, and to make us suspect all sorts of secret villainies that may never exist.

Men build their confidence on being personally treated with artificial delicacy. . . . At present men meet together with the temper less of friends than of enemies. Every man eyes his neighbour as if he expected to receive from him a secret wound. . . . How would the whole of this be reversed by the practice of sincerity? We could not be indifferent to men whose custom it was to tell us the truth. Hatred would perish, from a failure in its principal ingredient, the duplicity and impenetrableness of human actions.[1]

The last sentence is no doubt excessively optimistic; and we may smile when Godwin goes on: 'If there be, in the list of our acquaintance, any person we particularly dislike, it usually happens that it is for some moral fault. . . . Why should he be kept in ignorance of our opinion respecting him?'[2]

Most of us can think of several good reasons. But these characteristic excesses need not blind us to the merits of Godwin's case. These are quite good reasons for supposing that a society built on prestige and ambition will be less harmonious than Montesquieu supposed. Godwin has, actually, anticipated a good deal that modern psychologists and social anthropologists have said about such a society.

This is one of Godwin's two main reasons for rejecting the ideal of Honour. The other is his disbelief in the indirect paths to social harmony, advocated not only by Montesquieu but also by Hume and Bentham. However cunningly the

---

[1] *P.J.* i. 331–5.   [2] *P.J.* i. 366.

legislator may try to manipulate social institutions so that private vices will lead to public benefits, these arrangements are never quite foolproof. Situations may always occur in which the motives of ambition and avarice will conflict with the public good. If you want men to behave benevolently there is, in the long run, no substitute for benevolence.

But, although Godwin does not regard ambition, the desire for prestige, as a substitute for benevolence, he does realize that it is at least part of the cement by which society is held together. He makes this point in the essay *Of Personal Reputation* in *The Enquirer*, where he sums up: 'But, though reputation will never constitute, with a man of wisdom and virtue, the first and leading motive of his actions, it will certainly enter into his consideration.'[1] The society based on Honour is not, Godwin thinks, a good one; but the good society will be made possible, in part, by the thirst for prestige.

It must be admitted indeed, that the love of distinction appears, from experience and the past history of mankind, to have been their ruling passion. But the love of distinction is capable of different directions. At present, there is no more certain road to the general deference of mankind, than the exhibition of wealth. . . . But let us conceive this erroneous and pernicious estimate of things to be reversed. . . . Let us imagine the direct and unambiguous road to public esteem, to be the acquisition of talent, or the practice of virtue, the cultivation of some species of ingenuity, or the display of some generous and expansive sentiment. . . . This is merely, in other words, to suppose good sense, and clear and correct perceptions, at some time to gain the ascendency in the world.[2]

Godwin does not, then, suppose that ambition and the desire for prestige can, or indeed should, be rooted out of human nature altogether. He is content to point out that the

[1] *The Enquirer* (London, 1797), p. 281.   [2] *P.J.* ii. 427-8.

objects towards which this passion is directed vary considerably in different societies. He says indeed, to put it as a
modern sociologist might, that the object of prestige is a
'function' of the culture; which means, on Godwin's analysis
of society, a function of the political organization. But he
also assumes that some objects of prestige are the 'right' ones,
are really estimable; and the good society is the one in which
these are in fact esteemed. This is what is meant by seeing
things as they are. To substitute other objects for them may
be called the gospel of indirection.

There was indeed more than one version of the gospel of
indirection current in Godwin's time. As well as the theory of
Honour, there was the view, later made much of by the
laissez-faire economists, that the desire for material goods,
if left to itself, was capable of securing a harmonious and well-
regulated society. Godwin is quite prepared to play the first
of these against the second. In so doing, he anticipates
Veblen.

All men are accustomed to conceive a thirst after distinction
and pre-eminence, but they do not all fix upon wealth as the object
of this passion, but variously upon skill in any particular art, grace,
learning, talents, wisdom and virtue. . . . Wealth would be still
less capable of being mistaken for the universal passion, were it
not rendered by political institution, more than by its natural
influence, the road to honour and respect.[1]

This is just the point I have been discussing, that the object of prestige varies in, and with, different forms of society.
A little later he talks quite explicitly (though without using
the term) about conspicuous consumption:

The creditable artisan or tradesman exerts a certain species of
industry to supply his immediate wants. . . . But these are soon
supplied. The rest is exerted, that he may wear a better coat, that

[1] *P.J.* bk. v, ch. 13, vol. ii, pp. 111–12.

he may clothe his wife with gay attire, that he may have not merely a shelter, but a handsome habitation, not merely bread and flesh to eat, but that he may set it out with suitable decorum. How many of these things would engage his attention, if he lived on a desert island, and had no spectator of his economy? If we survey the appendages of our persons, there is scarcely an article that is not in some respect an appeal to the good will of our neighbours, or a refuge against their contempt.[1]

It is not necessary, then, to assume that society will always be limited by the defects of Economic Man. To suppose so is partly the result of regarding the common attitudes of our own time and place as cast-iron laws of human nature; and partly the result of a superficial analysis of even the motives operating in our own society. And, if it is not necessary, a society based on the profit motive is certainly not desirable. It fails, as the motive of Honour fails, because it is not reliable. If we want public benefits, we can never be sure of getting them from this private vice.

Both these points are made, in passing, in *St. Leon*. When St. Leon is thrown into prison, he imagines that, since he has unlimited wealth, he can bribe his way out of prison. Every man has his price; he need only keep on raising his bid. The Negro servant, Hector, refuses to take any bribe, out of simple honesty and loyalty. But Hector's master, the gaoler, is the Economic Man made flesh: in Godwin's words, 'his avarice had swallowed up all his other passions'. He takes the bribe, but does not keep his side of the bargain. The profit motive, that is to say, is not always dominant; and even when it is, it cannot always be channelled in the desired direction.

Later, when he is seized by the Inquisition, St. Leon finds another incorruptible, in the inquisitor, but one whose motives are very different from Hector's.

[1] *P.J.* ii. 426.

. . . he would yet have regarded every doubloon he received as the price of his continual adversity here and damnation hereafter. I gained nothing favourable for my situation by the trial I had made, but I added a new chapter to my knowledge of human nature. I found that to be a knave it was not necessary to be an infidel: I corrected the too hasty conclusion which I had adopted with the rest of my contemporaries, that he whose conduct was infamous must inevitably be destitute of religious impressions and conceit; and I became satisfied that a man, while he practised every vice that can disgrace human nature, might imagine he was doing God a service.[1]

This is, of course, a third version of the gospel of indirection and a very influential one; it had received at least the partial blessing of almost all the most respected moralists of the past: for example, Locke, Berkeley, and even Bishop Butler. All these would have agreed that fear of God's punishments both is, and ought to be, the prime motive for virtuous actions. We are inclined to forget how widespread this view was in the seventeenth and eighteenth centuries. In its fullest development it becomes a kind of theistic Hobbism; indeed its exponents out-Hobbes Hobbes. For Hobbes has two (not quite consistent) answers to the question: why should we obey the civil ruler? He does say, at times, 'because the ruler has power to punish us'; but he devotes much more space to his second answer, which is: 'because obeying the civil ruler is in accordance with natural law' (in his very special sense of the term). And he does try to reduce the first answer to the second: to show that the power of punishment derives from natural law. These more orthodox exponents of natural law, on the other hand, turn out on examination to be saying that civil law is subordinate to divine law simply because God has greater power to cause us pain or pleasure than the government. That is, they reduce

[1] *St. Leon*, iii. 235.

the authority of the natural law to the power to punish. God is the super-Leviathan.

We have already discussed Godwin's attitude to this doctrine in Chapter 1. Here it is only necessary to say that he rejects it for the same two reasons as he rejects Honour or the profit motive. The motive does not always operate; and when it does it will not necessarily result in virtuous actions. Belief in God's punishments or rewards is indeed especially likely to fail, because it can only have the force of a rule of thumb, not of *scientia intuitiva*. Godwin, indeed, uses it as an illustration of the difference between the two:

It is so different a thing to conceive a proposition theoretically, and to experience it in practice! The case is parallel to that of the expectation which an ordinary Christian entertains of eternal bliss. It is an article in his creed; he repeats it every night when he lies down, and every morning when he rises. He would be both offended and surprised if you told him he was not persuaded of it; and yet how faint and indistinct a picture it produces in his intellectual retina! The affairs of this world strike him with all the force of vision; to them he cannot make himself a stranger and a pilgrim; he cannot transfer all his affections to the mere creature of his imagination, engendered in solitude and nurtured by enthusiasm, heaven.[1]

But there may be men, like the inquisitor, in whom the motive does not fail. And here the motive is unreliable in the other sense; it need not prevent them from 'practising every vice that can disgrace human nature'. The orthodox view was that, since God is benevolent, He must be presumed to reward those who do good to others and punish those who do not. Hence the fear of God will, in practice, ensure benevolent behaviour. But it was usual to add, as Butler did, that men must not trust their own imperfect calculations of the effect of their actions on human happiness. It was much

[1] *St. Leon*, iv. 7. And see *P.J.* ii. 127–8.

safer to consider only the direct commands of God, as conveyed to us by our consciences. Obviously the conscience of the inquisitor is very relevant here; and it was only necessary for Godwin to point to him to show that this indirect method of securing benevolent behaviour was as unreliable as the other two.

The upshot of it all is this: if man is as he has been represented, if he is only capable of being moved by self-interest in some form or other, then his case is hopeless. It is not possible, that is to say, to have a happy and harmonious society. Hume was wrong when he said: 'It is . . . a just political maxim, that every man must be supposed to be a knave'; the programme of Mandeville, or of Montesquieu (*il se trouve que chacun va au bien commun, croyant aller à ses intérêts particuliers*) is doomed to failure.

5

THE DEPRAVITY OF VIRTUE

SINCE Godwin rejects the ideal of Honour, we might expect him to plump for Virtue and the noble austerities of the Republic. This was the usual inspiration of reformers in his time. Montesquieu seems to have performed the unique feat of furnishing one set of theoretical arguments for conservatives and another for radicals.

There can be no doubt that Godwin was much more sympathetic to the republican ideal. For one thing, it demanded equality; and Godwin was quite sure that equality was necessary if men were to see each other as they really were. Montesquieu had said that a republic was only possible in a tiny state; and Godwin felt strongly that communities should be kept small in order to limit the need for rules of thumb. You cannot hope to see your neighbour as he really is if you have millions of neighbours.

The republican ideal had inspired the common eighteenth-century denunciations of luxury. As we have seen, Godwin had some sympathy with these; but he did not accept the thesis that poverty was, in its own right, the nurse of virtue and happiness. We have seen that he criticizes this view explicitly in *Mandeville*. In *Political Justice* he points out that the term 'luxury' was badly in need of definition. We may confirm this by observing the flounderings of the Reverend John Adams. Adams begins by noticing that in the fourteenth-century chimneys were regarded as luxuries, and tells a story of a Highlander who rebuked his son for effeminacy because, sleeping out in the snow, he used a snowball as a pillow. He goes on to give 'the true definition of luxury', viz.: 'a faulty excess in the gratification of the external senses'. Obviously, this leaves the problem pretty much where it was; and it does not really help much to be told that 'what excess in such pleasures is faulty is not difficult to determine' (being condemned by the moral sense), or that 'faulty' here means 'hurtful to the mind or body'.[1] Adams himself thinks that 'down-beds, soft pillows, and easy seats' are to be condemned, because they 'tend to enervate the body'; so are coaches, which enervate both body and mind, whereas riding on horseback, 'though a less vigorous exertion of strength than walking, is not luxury, because it is a healthful exercise'.[2] He also says that Voltaire was wrong to regard wearing shoes as luxury, though this would seem to fit his criterion perfectly. And he adds, quite significantly: 'To consider luxury in a political view, no refinement of dress, of the table, of equipage, of habitation, is luxury in those who can afford the expense; and the public gains by the encouragement that is given to arts, manufactures and commerce.'[2] Nevertheless, 'luxury has been the ruin of every state where it prevailed', because it 'opens a wide door to indolence, sensuality, corruption, prostitution, perdition', and it is 'above all, pernicious in a commercial state'.

This seems an extraordinary muddle; and it probably reflects fairly clearly the popular confusion of mind on the subject. Adams has given us a confused version of the republican objection to luxury, which was twofold. Luxury made the citizen unfit in body, and so unable or unwilling to defend his country in war; and unfit in mind, because he cared more for his personal possessions than for the body politic.

Godwin's position is quite different.

If we understand by a luxury, something which is to be enjoyed exclusively by some, at the expense of undue privations, and a partial burthen upon others; to indulge ourselves in luxury is then a vice. But, if we understand by luxury, which is frequently

---

[1] *Curious Thoughts on the History of Man*, ch. 50.
[2] Ibid., pp. 146–7.

the case, every accommodation which is not absolutely necessary to maintain us in sound and healthful existence, the procuring and communicating luxuries may then be virtuous. The end of virtue is to add to the sum of pleasurable sensation.[1]

Godwin's objection to luxury, then, is not in the least an ascetic one. Nor is he worried about the citizen's attention being distracted from something called the State. He is concerned simply with the question of social justice. Let no one eat cake until everyone has bread; at any rate let no one eat cake if someone else is made a drudge by the baking of it. But there is no particular objection to cake as such. Godwin's ideal is not an ascetic one, and he is not really a simple-lifer. He would have agreed with Bernard Shaw that the thing to do is to bury poverty, not to praise it.

In the essay *Of Avarice and Profusion* that provoked Malthus, Godwin argues that the miser is of more value to society than the spendthrift. Here and there in the essay he seems to be talking the language of asceticism. Thus he says of the miser:

He strips the world of its gaudy plumage, and views it in its genuine colours. He estimates splendid equipages and costly attire exactly, or nearly, at their true value. He feels with acute sensibility the folly of wasting the wealth of a province upon a meal. He knows that a man may be as alert, as vigorous, and as happy, whose food is the roots of the earth and whose drink the running streams.[2]

But Godwin is (rather surprisingly) being playful here. He is making out a case for the miser, with his tongue in his cheek, much as writers like Mandeville had made out a case for the spendthrift. This becomes obvious when he goes on, in the next paragraph:

It is true indeed that he exaggerates his principles. . . . His system would not only drive out of the world that luxury, which

---

[1] *P.J.* ii. 492–3.   [2] *The Enquirer* (London, 1797), p. 181.

unnerves and debases the men that practice it. . . . It would destroy painting, and music and the splendour of public exhibitions. Literature itself would languish under its frigid empire. But our censure would be extensive indeed, if we condemned every enthusiast of any science or principle, who exaggerated its maxims.

In the essay as a whole it is not the ascetic but the socialist objection to luxury that is stressed.

There is no wealth in the world except this, the labour of man. What is misnamed wealth, is merely a power vested in certain individuals by the institutions of society, to compel others to labour for their benefit. So much labour is required to produce the necessaries of life; so much more to produce those super-fluities which at present exist in any country. Every new luxury is a new weight thrown into the scale. The poor are scarcely ever benefited by this. It adds a certain portion to the mass of their labour; but it adds nothing to their conveniences.[1]

In the world as it is, luxury is to be avoided, because it adds to the burdens of the poor; but in the world as it might be, luxury, regarded simply as an additional source of pleasure, is to be commended. It is true that Godwin adds (and it is here that he comes closest to asceticism) that many so-called luxuries turn out in practice to be hardly worth the labour of making them. At the same time, he insists that the kind of man we should aim at producing will need a good many things that are beyond the reach of the poor. Even if he eats bread and cheese and drinks water (and Godwin does not say that he will) he will certainly want books, painting, musical instruments. He will also need to feel secure. St. Leon, who tries for a time to lead the simple life in Switzerland, finds that his calm is rudely shattered by a storm which ruins the crops of an entire district.

I have spoken of the 'ascetic' objection to luxury. But this

---

[1] *The Enquirer*, p. 177.

is an ambiguous term which may refer either to the republican or to the primitivist objection. The republican objection,
as I have said, is that luxuries distract a man's attention from
his duty to his country, and soften him so that he cannot fight
for it. The primitivist objection is based on the assumption
that man is naturally good, and has been corrupted by civilization. It is through luxury that he becomes corrupted. The
two positions are often confused, even by those who hold
them; but there is an important difference. The citizen of the
republic, the ideal Spartan or Roman, is very much a product
of his society. You do not make such a citizen by leaving man
in his 'natural' state. Indeed, the republic has to keep a watch-
ful eye on him to see that he does attain the required standard
of 'virtue'.

I am suggesting that Godwin does not hold either of these
objections to luxury. It is true that he does hold, in a sense,
that men are corrupted by society. Wrong actions spring from
wrong opinions, and wrong opinions are socially engendered.
But so, in a way, are right ones. Right opinions, it is true,
come from seeing things as they are; and it might be thought
that to achieve this, it is only necessary to remove the blinkers
of prejudice. Godwin does sometimes talk in this strain.   But
he makes it quite clear, all the same, that it is only the cultivated man who is able to see things as they are. 'The pleasures
I would pursue and disseminate', it will be remembered, 'are
such as could not be understood by the rustic and the savage.'
And Godwin thought this point important enough to include
it in the summary of principles at the beginning of *Political
Justice*. 'This state (i.e. the most desirable state of man) is a
state of high civilization.'

The man without prejudice is as much a social product as
the man of prejudice. The difference between them depends
on the distinction between indoctrination and education. You
indoctrinate with prejudice; you educate people to see the

truth. The distinction is not without its difficulties; but Godwin is certainly not alone in wishing to maintain it. If it can be maintained, what he has to say about society seems reasonable enough.

So far I have argued that Godwin's objections to luxury are not the republican objections. What is much more important is that the republican 'virtue' is not really a state in which men see things as they are. The citizen of the republic has been indoctrinated even more assiduously than the Man of Honour.

There is a good deal of evidence that Godwin had the *Esprit des Lois* specially in mind when he wrote *St. Leon*. I have already suggested that St. Leon, like Falkland, is the Man of Honour. Further, each of the three types of state is described there in language which might have come straight from Montesquieu. The bashaw of Hungary objects to St. Leon's philanthropic projects as being in conflict with the principle of a despotic state:

Know, sir, that, through the whole extent of his dominions, there is but one proprietor, and that is our illustrious monarch. You say, that you wish to be the benefactor of his subjects, and the judge of your own proceedings; such sentiments are flat rebellion against the glorious constitution of Ottoman. The sovereign of Constantinople will have no benefactor in the countries he presides over, but himself. Like the invisible ruler of the universe, he acts by second causes; he allows his ministers to be the instruments of his beneficence; but all must be ascribed to him, must flow from his will, must be placed under his control.[1]

The other two polities provide dramatic contrast when St. Leon, the Man of Honour, is haled before a Swiss magistrate on suspicion of the murder of the mysterious stranger who bequeathed him the philosopher's stone and the secret of

---

[1] *St. Leon* (London, 1799), iv. 95.

immortality. The only actual evidence against him is his sudden access of wealth.

I cannot collect from anything you have said that I have an accuser or that any charge has been alleged against me. Till that happens, I cannot fall under your animadversion. I am a man of generous birth and honourable sentiments. To myself and my own conscience only am I accountable for my expenditure and my income. I disdain to answer to any tribune on earth an enquiry of this sort. . . .

You are mistaken, sir [said the magistrate]. What you mention may be the rule of administering justice in some states. They may decide, if they think proper, that some open act, apparently of a criminal description, must be alleged against a man, before he can become an object of animadversion to the state. But in Constance, as I have already told you, the government assumes to act the part of a parent to its subjects. I sit here, not merely to investigate and examine definite acts, but as a *censor morum*; and I should commit a breach of the oath of my office, if I did not lend a vigilant attention to the behaviour and conduct of every one within my jurisdiction. The city of Constance requires that nothing immoral, licentious or of suspicious character, shall be transacted within its walls. Your proceedings have escaped notice too long. . . .[1]

This is precisely the republican attitude to legal procedure as Montesquieu describes it. Now it might be thought that Godwin would not find this altogether uncongenial. He had his own objections, as we have seen, to the reign of law. He agreed that it was important to the State that every citizen should have right opinions. Indeed, almost the whole object of the State was to provide the conditions that would lead to the subject's having right opinions. Godwin did not, of course, believe that the citizen should sacrifice his own welfare to that of 'the State', conceived as something apart from the individuals comprising it; but he did believe that the citizen

[1] *St. Leon*, ii. 258–9.

should sink his own happiness in the greatest happiness of the greatest number. He also believed that no action was, properly speaking, indifferent.

Morality is nothing else but that system, which teaches us to contribute upon all occasions, to the extent of our power, to the well-being and happiness of every intellectual and sensitive existence. But there is no action of our lives, which does not in some way affect that happiness. There is not one of our avocations or amusements, that does not, by its effects, render us more or less fit to contribute our quota to the general utility.[1]

This would seem to be precisely what the magistrate of Constance is saying. And Godwin does indeed argue, in the same chapter of *Political Justice*, that the individual has, in a sense, no rights, There are, in the conduct of our lives, no reserved areas which do not concern our neighbours, and in which they must not meddle. Indeed,

our neighbour . . . is guilty of an omission . . . if he fail to employ every means in his power for the amendment of our errors, and to have recourse for that purpose, as he may see occasion, to the most unreserved animadversion upon our propensities and conduct. It is absurd to suppose that certain points are especially within my province, and therefore he may not afford me, invited or uninvited, his assistance in arriving at a right decision. . . . The worst consequences, through every rank and department of life, have arisen, from men's supposing their personal affairs in any case to be so sacred, that every one, except themselves, was bound to be blind and dumb in relation to them.[2]

So far, then, Godwin may seem to approve of that typically republican institution, the *censor morum*. But he differs from the magistrate of Constance in one very important particular. I have a duty to show my neighbour the error of his ways, and to set him on the right path, 'invited or uninvited'; but I must

[1] *P.J.*, ii, ch. 5, vol. i, p. 159.　　　　[2] Ibid., pp. 162–3.

not use any form of coercion. For, although Godwin expressly asserts his disagreement with Tom Paine, and will not concede the rights to life and liberty ('Other men are bound ... to deprive him of life or liberty, if that should appear in any case to be indispensably necessary to prevent a greater evil'),[1] it turns out that the individual has one right, after all: the right of private judgement. 'Every man has a certain sphere of discretion, which he has a right to expect shall not be infringed by his neighbours.'[1]

At first sight this looks like a flat contradiction. What is 'a sphere of discretion', if it is not a reserved area in which others may not meddle? Was St. Leon right or wrong when he insisted: 'To myself and my own conscience only am I accountable for my expenditure and my income'?

Godwin's answer is that he was wrong if he supposed that these matters did not concern his neighbours. They did. They had, therefore, not so much a right as a duty to give St. Leon their opinion of his conduct; but they were not entitled to go further than giving advice.

Every man has a certain sphere of discretion which he has a right to expect shall not be infringed by his neighbours. This right flows from the very nature of man. First, all men are fallible: no man can be justified in setting up his judgment as a standard for others. . . . If every one be desirous of imposing his sense upon others, it will at last come to a controversy, not of reason, but of force. Secondly, even if we had an infallible criterion, nothing would be gained, unless it were by all men recognised as such. If I were secured against the possibility of mistake, mischief and not good would accrue, from imposing my infallible truths upon my neighbour, and requiring his submission independently of any conviction I could produce in his understanding. Man is a being who can never be an object of just approbation, any further than he is independent. He must consult his own reason, draw his own conclusions, and conscientiously conform himself to his ideas of

[1] Ibid., p. 167.

propriety. Without this, he will be neither active, nor considerate, nor resolute, nor generous.[1]

This is not unlike Mill's *On Liberty*; and we may regard this as showing, once again, that Godwin thought like the later utilitarians; certainly he is here closer to the utilitarians than to those contemporaries of his who talked about the Rights of Man. But it may be asked of Godwin, as it has been asked of Mill, whether this position is really compatible with utilitarianism. Godwin seems to be arguing that you cannot make a man virtuous by Act of Parliament. But does it matter, on utilitarian principles, whether he is 'an object of just approbation' or not, provided he is useful to his neighbours?

Godwin's answer is implicit in the last sentence of the passage just quoted. You cannot really rely on the man who does the right thing for the wrong motive. Circumstances may always arise in which he will let you down. And this applies to 'virtue', or public spirit, as much as to 'honour', or ambition. The republican theory of the State is, in short, just another version of the gospel of indirection.

But why is public spirit not the right motive? What is public spirit, after all, but a regard for the welfare of my neighbours? And Godwin insists on this, again and again, as the most important of our duties.

Part of Godwin's reply to this objection is, of course, notorious. We need only remind ourselves of the Archbishop's chambermaid. Patriotism teaches us to restrict our benevolence to our own countrymen; and their welfare may well conflict with the larger happiness of mankind. It is true that Godwin had modified his opinion about this; but only so far as to introduce the division of labour argument, made much of by the later utilitarians. The general happiness will be best served if each of us concentrates on the happiness of rela-

[1] *P.J.* i. 167–8.

tively few individuals: we can do much for them, little for mankind in general. 'This is the great distribution of human society', says one of the characters in *Fleetwood*. 'Every one who stands in need of assistance appertains to some one individual, upon whom he has a stronger claim than upon any other of his fellow creatures. My son belongs to me, because I was the occasion of his coming into existence; you belong to me, because you were hungry and I fed you, because you wanted education and a protector and have found them in me.'[1]

It will be seen that the real son has no greater claim than the adopted one. It is convenient to recognize the ties of blood, but this is a mere matter of convenience; my obligation to my friends and family derive from my obligation to mankind in general. If the two claims conflict, I should still prefer the greater sum of happiness: Godwin has not really said anything to upset this conclusion. Even in *St. Leon*, the book in which Godwin was to correct what he had said about 'domestic and private affections', he makes it clear that they can conflict with public ones. In the preface he praises the domestic affections on the grounds that they are in themselves a source of happiness, and that they are, moreover, 'likely to render (us) more prompt in the service of strangers and the public'. But he does not say that they will always do this; and in the novel itself there is a curious Gothic character, Bethlem Gabor, who becomes a misanthrope because of the death of his wife and children. 'He never saw a festive board without an inclination to overturn it; or a father encircled with a smiling family, without feeling his soul thrill with suggestions of murder. . . . I knew that all the unsocial propensities that now animated him, were the offspring of love, were the sentiments of a lioness bereaved of her young.'[2]

But Bethlem Gabor has lost his family; and the point may be that that it is only possible to feel universal benevolence

---

[1] *Fleetwood* (London, 1805), ii. 52–53.   [2] *St. Leon*, iv. 128–9.

while one is also surrounded by purely personal love and affection. This seems to be the theme of *Fleetwood*; Fleetwood is a misanthrope because he has never been able to find a true friend. What Godwin is saying, I think, is that love and friendship awaken the feelings that make the passion of universal benevolence possible; but it is still important to see that these feelings are not too narrowly channelled. It is still necessary, then, to see that narrow loyalties are not stressed at the expense of wider ones; and this is precisely what the ideal of 'virtue' does. To love one's fellow countrymen for the sake of one's 'country' is still to do the right thing for the wrong reason; love of country, then, is still an unreliable motive. This point comes out in *St. Leon* when St. Leon finds that his philanthropic attempts to relieve famine in Hungary are bitterly resented by his own son:

To the eternal disgrace of the nation that gave him birth, he had joined the Turkish standard, and, by exertions difficult to be comprehended, had rescued the infidels from famine at a time when, but for his inauspicious interference, Buda, and perhaps every strong town in Hungary, were on the point of falling into the hands of the emperor.[1]

But this is not all. Love for one's country may not only make one unjust to foreigners; it may make one neglect the real welfare of one's countrymen in favour of an unreal abstraction called national honour. The Spartans, after all, served their country at the expense of their countrymen. There is a passage in *Political Justice* in which Godwin expressly contrasts his own attitude to the nation with that of Rousseau and his supporters. He offers us a paraphrase of the republican sentiment:

Their perpetual exhortation has been, 'Love your country. Sink the personal existence of individuals in the existence of the com-

---

[1] *St. Leon*, iv. 222.

munity. Make little account of the particular men of whom the society consists, but aim at the general wealth, prosperity and glory. Purify your mind from the gross ideas of sense, and elevate it to the single contemplation of that abstract individual, of which particular men are so many detached members, valuable only for the place they fill.

Godwin goes on:

The lessons of reason on this head are different from these. 'Society is an ideal existence, and not, on its own account, entitled to the smallest regard. The wealth, prosperity and glory of the whole are unintelligible chimeras. Set no value on any thing, but in proportion as you are convinced of its tendency to make individual men happy and virtuous. Benefit, by every practicable mode, man wherever he exists; but be not deceived by the specious idea of affording services to a body of men, for which no individual man is the better. Society was constituted, not for the sake of glory, not to furnish splendid materials for the page of history, but for the benefit of its members. The love of our country, as the term has usually been understood, has too often been found to be one of those specious illusions, which are employed by impostors, for the purpose of rendering the multitude the blind instruments of their crooked designs.'[1]

Godwin here comes quite close to those modern philosophers who regard terms like 'nation' as 'systematically misleading expressions'. Any sentence containing such a word needs, as it were, to be translated before we can really see what it means. We need to restate an assertion about a nation in terms of the individuals comprising it. In another chapter[2] he points out that it is inaccurate to speak of 'young' and 'old' nations in the sense in which we apply these terms to individuals. This confusion, he suggests, is bound up with 'romantic notions of pastoral life and the golden age'; and gives rise to the fallacy that a nation can be 'sunk into

[1] *P.J.* ii. 145–6.   [2] *P.J.*, bk. i, ch. 7, vol. i, pp. 105–9.

decrepitude', so that any reform is hopeless. Here again Godwin probably has Rousseau in mind.[1]

The objection to the republican ideal, then, is that it encourages such fallacies. It prevents men from seeing things as they are by turning their attention away from human beings towards mythical entities. Here in short we have another source of prejudices, or rules of thumb. To substitute 'my duty to my country' for 'my duty to my neighbour' is only a little less dangerous than to substitute 'my duty to my monarch' or 'my sense of honour' or 'my duty to God'. All these, in their different ways, lead men astray. There is no substitute for benevolence based on a sympathetic understanding of the way men think and feel.

There is, indeed, a passage in Godwin's *Life of Chaucer* that suggests that, if Godwin had to choose between the republican and the monarchic ideals, he might, after all, choose 'Honour':

It is principally to the feudal system that we owe the distinguishing features of modern, as contrasted with ancient Europe, that we belong more to our families and less to the state, that we are more of men and less of machines. The great chain of subordination in the feudal law, has generated among and entailed upon us a continual respect to the combinations and affections which bind man to man, and neighbour to neighbour. We are no longer broken down to one level, and into one mass, under the unsympathising and insensible government of institutions and edicts; but live in unforced intercourse, one with another, and consult much oftener the dictates of feeling and promptings of disposition, than the inventions of legislators. The consequence of this is, that we remark and treasure a thousand little sentiments and emotions, which the ancients deemed below or foreign to their consideration; and our characters, cherished by the warmth of a less artificial mode of society, unfold a variety of minuter lineaments and features, which under other circumstances in man have

[1] See *The Social Contract*, bk. ii, ch. 8.

been blighted and destroyed. The feudal system was the nurse of chivalry, and the parent of romance; and out of these have sprung the principle of modern honour in the best sense of that term, the generosity of disinterested adventure, and the more persevering and successful cultivation of the private affections.[1]

Part of the objection to republicanism, then, is that it appeals to an emotion (patriotism) and a set of concepts (the nation, national honour, national glory, &c.) that between them distort men's judgement of things as they are. This distortion is made worse by the institutions to which republicanism gives rise, or at least by the one on which Rousseau pins so many hopes, the national assembly.

Godwin finds his first objection to national assemblies[2] in what Rousseau had considered their chief virtue. National assemblies force men to compromise. Or, as Godwin put it,

they produce a fictitious unanimity. . . . The individuals who constitute a nation, cannot take into consideration a variety of important questions, without forming different sentiments respecting them. In reality, all questions that are brought before such an assembly, are decided by a majority of votes, and the minority, after having exposed, with all the power of eloquence, and force of reasoning, of which they are capable, the injustice and folly of the measures adopted, are obliged, in a certain sense, to assist in carrying them into execution. Nothing can more directly contribute to the depravation of the human understanding and character.

Rousseau had said, on the contrary, that the need to compromise in this way led to man's salvation, since it led him to substitute the public interest, the general will, for his private interest or particular will. In order to see what is at issue between him and Godwin we need to notice an ambiguity in this concept of compromise.

[1] William Godwin, *Life of Geoffrey Chaucer* (London, 1803), i. 360–1.
[2] In the chapter 'Of National Assemblies' in *P.J.*, bk. v, ch. 23.

It is not always clear, in Rousseau, whether the individual is to vote for his own immediate interest or for what he conceives to be the general interest. If he votes for his own interest (or at least for the general rule that best embodies his own interest), then we may concede Rousseau's point that particular interests will cancel each other out, and that the rule favoured by the majority will at least embody the largest number of interests. The 'general will' then becomes something like the greatest happiness of the greatest number, and to say that the individual should accept the general will as his own is to say that he should recognize the justice of preferring the general happiness to his own individual happiness. And this may be what Rousseau means when he says, in a puzzling passage: 'When therefore the opinion that is contrary to my own prevails, this proves neither more nor less than that I was mistaken, and that what I thought to be the general will was not so. If my particular opinion had carried the day I should have achieved the opposite of what was my will; and it is in that case that I should not have been free'.[1] Rousseau may mean simply that the conscientious citizen would not want his own interest to prevail against that of the majority. In which case, of course, Godwin would entirely agree with him.

But it is at least doubtful whether 'what I thought to be the general will was not so' can bear this interpretation. And Rousseau does seem to say, at least in some passages, that we should vote, not for our own interests, but for what we conceive to be the general interest. Now this alters the case entirely, and makes it no longer obvious that I should accept the decision if it goes against me. Take a parallel case. Let us suppose a competition in which competitors are asked to vote for the ten most popular books of the century. There is a prize, which goes to the competitor whose list most nearly coincides with the choice of the majority. Can the result fairly

[1] *Social Contract*, bk. iv, ch. 2.

be called the ten most popular books? It can, if each competitor votes for the books he himself likes best. But if he
votes for the books he imagines to appeal most to his fellow
competitors (as of course he will, in an attempt to win the
prize), then we are not entitled to say that the winning list
tells us what books are most popular, but only what books
most people think to be most popular. And we may well be
mistaken about our neighbour's tastes, if not about our own.
In exactly the same way, there is no need to suppose that the
majority is the best judge of the public interest, even if we
suppose every man to be the best judge of his own. It is one
thing to compromise in order to take account of the declared
wishes of my neighbour; quite another to compromise with a
third person's opinion of what those wishes are. I think that
Rousseau argues that the general will is infallible because he
does not distinguish clearly between these two.

But of course we do not solve the problem by saying simply
that everyone should vote for the general rule which he thinks
will best serve his own interests. This may result in our knowing the interest of the majority (assuming, what is not at all
certain, that everyone is the best judge of his own interest)
but it still does not give us the greatest happiness of the
greatest number; for, of course, the sufferings of the minority
may outweigh some relatively slight advantage to the majority.
There is, then, no escape from trying to judge the general
happiness directly; and this means that the decision of the
national assembly may well be wrong.

Godwin does not put the case in this way; but he does
insist strongly on the fallibility of the majority, and, as we
have seen, on the evil effects of making the minority support
a policy which they believe to be wrong. It is easy to misunder-
stand Godwin here, and to be impatient with him. How, we
naturally ask, are such matters to be decided if not by majority
vote, and how is government possible at all if those who are

outvoted do not acquiesce in the decision? But this is a different point, and one which Godwin concedes. 'That any man, or body of men, should impose their sense upon persons of a different opinion is, absolutely speaking, wrong, and in all cases deeply to be regretted: but this evil it is perhaps in some degree necessary to incur, for the sake of a preponderating good. All government includes in it this evil, as one of its fundamental characteristics.'[1]

Acquiescence in the majority decision is, then, necessary to government: Godwin does not deny that. But his point is that it is a necessary evil, not, as Rousseau and others had believed, a good. We must not identify this process with the very different one by which the individual comes to identify his fellows' good with his own. That, Godwin would say, is the fundamental error of those who praised the republican ideal.

Why is acquiescence an evil? Godwin would not, of course, deny that we should pay very careful attention to the opinions of others, and that we should always be ready to believe that our own opinions may be mistaken. He urges both these points strongly in the essay 'Of Difference in Opinion' in *The Enquirer*, where he applies them especially to political differences. And, of course, he believes that debate and discussion are among the more important means of coming to see things as they are. Nor is his point only that the political debates of legislative assemblies are rarely disinterested. He does indeed point out all the usual objections to deliberative assemblies. Some of these had been acknowledged by Rousseau: notably the bad effects of party intrigue. Rousseau thought he could guard against these defects by eliminating parties and pressure groups of every kind; but Godwin argues, with some cogency, that the mere fact of taking a vote is enough to deprive the debates of any real value.

[1] *P.J.* i. 259.

Debate and discussion are, in their own nature, highly conducive to intellectual improvement; but they lose this salutary
character, the moment they are subjected to this unfortunate condition. What can be more unreasonable, than to demand, that
argument, the usual quality of which is gradually and impercep-
tibly to enlighten the mind, should declare its effect in the close of a
single conversation? No sooner does this circumstance occur, than
the whole scene loses its character. The orator no longer enquires
after permanent conviction, but transitory effect. He seeks rather
to take advantage of our prejudices, than to enlighten our judgment. That which might otherwise have been a scene of patient
and beneficient enquiry, is changed into wrangling, tumult and
precipitation.[1]

He goes on to assert that assemblies are on the whole less wise
than individuals, both because the individual no longer feels
the same personal responsibility for the decision, and because
the leaders have to pander to the prejudices of their followers.
These are real defects in democratic institutions, and we
should recognize the strength of Godwin's case here. But his
real point is quite a different one, and would remain even if it
could be shown that national assemblies are invariably wise
and just.

It is better, Godwin says, for men to obey out of fear than
out of trust in the superior wisdom of those with whom they
disagree.

Comply, where the necessity of the case demands it; but criticise
while you comply. . . . Obey; this may be right; but beware of
reverence. . . . Whatever I submit to from the irresistible impulse
of necessity, is not mine, and debases me only as it tends gradually
to shackle the intrepidity of my character. . . . But, where I make
the voluntary surrender of my understanding, and commit my
conscience to another man's keeping. . . . I then become the most
mischievous and pernicious of animals. . . . I am the ready tool of
injustice, cruelty and profligacy.[2]

[1] *P.J.* ii. 203–4.   [2] *P.J.*, bk. iii, ch. 6, vol. i, pp. 230–3.

Godwin has, I think, two points here, though he may not always distinguish them clearly. It is bad for the citizen to acquiesce in something which he strongly believes to be wrong; but it is also bad for him to acquiesce in something about which he has no very strong feelings, one way or the other. If I do either of these I may be said to commit my conscience to another man's keeping. We are inclined to agree with Godwin about the first, but not about the second. Why shouldn't the citizen leave matters of state to the experts, doing his own duty by co-operating cheerfully in whatever they ask of him, provided they ask nothing that does violence to his own conscience?

There is, Godwin would say, a very good reason; it is precisely this procedure that gives rise to rules of thumb. It is, after all, a commonplace that nations behave much worse than individuals. In the twentieth century men who would not, in their private capacity, hurt a fly, may inflict the most bestial cruelties when ordered to by their governments; tearing the limbs off children with high explosives, or burning men and women alive. They can do these things because they have learned to surrender their consciences to other men's keeping. They do not feel responsibility for these actions as individuals. Indeed, they hardly recognize them for what they are. They do not think of themselves as torturing other men and women, but as 'doing their bit', or 'softening enemy resistance', or whatever the euphemism of the moment may be. It is in this way that rules of thumb blind men to things as they are. And one can see what Godwin means when he says that the pacifist who yields to force and does these things against his will, while hating them and resisting them as much as he can, is less harmed, fundamentally, than the ordinary well-meaning citizen who accepts them as his duty because he trusts his rulers.

So far we have been considering the citizen who is asked to

do something that is actually evil, whether or not he thinks it is. But the results are hardly less unfortunate, Godwin would say, when he acquiesces in a measure that is actually good. For the truth is that Godwin is not concerned with the need to take practical decisions about the day-to-day problems of government, and to abide by these decisions once they are taken. He is thinking of the long-term effects of those decisions in moulding the institutions that mould men's minds. The point is not so much that governments make laws as that they create attitudes. And the attitudes may be wrong, even if the laws are right. Indeed, the attitudes are bound to be wrong so long as the laws are accepted unthinkingly; for 'he that believes the most fundamental proposition, through the influence of authority, does not believe a truth but a falsehood'.

Since this is the core of Godwin's whole political theory, it is important to see what he meant. Let us take an example. In comparatively recent times successive measures have been passed increasing income tax, so that the individual's contribution to public funds is now, by the standard of a hundred or even fifty years ago, fantastically high. These measures have generally been opposed, often quite bitterly; but the opponents have been in a minority, and have consequently had to acquiesce. One result of this has no doubt been that taxes have been paid grudgingly, and often evaded; but there is another result, less noticed, and not very easy to detect. Gradually even the opponents of taxation have come to accept it as right and proper; only it is not quite right and proper, because the attitudes which led them to oppose it in the first place still persist. They still believe that a man should be able to do what he likes with his own earnings, and that the distribution of income is best settled by the working of economic laws, and should not be artificially regulated by the Government. But they have also come to believe that the State should provide social services financed from taxation;

and of course this does actually effect a redistribution of income and seriously limit the right of individual spending. We see here the birth of a typical rule of thumb, or, as Godwin puts it, a proposition that is believed without being understood.

This is I think what Godwin means when he speaks of the acquiescence of the outvoted resulting in 'the depravation of the human understanding, and character'. It is, first and foremost, the understanding that is depraved. Eventually, as the result of many such compromises, our minds become a muddle: the kind of muddle that the Lynds found when they investigated the attitudes of typical citizens of Middletown. They found that men commonly held, at the same time, such inconsistent beliefs as:

> Hard work and thrift are signs of character and the way to get ahead.
>
> No shrewd person tries to get ahead nowadays just by working hard, and nobody gets rich nowadays by pinching nickels. If you want to make money, you have to look and act like money.

It seems a little hard to blame democratic institutions for such inconsistencies. But it can be argued, plausibly enough, that the muddle here results from a conflict between two sets of institutions.[1] The belief in hard work and thrift was appropriate in an economy based on the small independent craftsman. What has happened in America is that this economy has been replaced by a very different one without any corresponding change in the *official* ideology. Hence the opposing beliefs jostle each other uneasily in the popular mind. That, at any rate, is Thurman Arnold's contention. Whether or not we accept it entirely,[2] it gives us a good example of the way

[1] See Thurman W. Arnold, *The Folklore of Capitalism* (New Haven, Yale University Press, 1937).

[2] I have attempted some criticism of it in 'The Concept of Myth' in *The Sociological Review*, xlii, 1950, section 6.

in which an institution, once it is accepted in practice, will generate a belief. If it is never fully accepted in theory, the result will be a mental muddle.

But, it may be objected, modern capitalism has just grown; it has not been created deliberately by government fiat. Probably Godwin, like most of his contemporaries, attributed too much to the direct effect of legislative action; but at least it can be said that the acquiescence of the outvoted minority is one case (though not the only or perhaps even the commonest case) of an institution being accepted in practice but not in theory. The situation can, then, give rise to this kind of muddle; and for Godwin, it must be remembered, mental muddle is the root of all evil.

It is significant that Godwin, in a footnote, praises Rousseau for *Émile*, but adds: 'In his writings expressly political, *Du contrat social* and *Considérations sur la Pologne*, the superiority of his genius seems to desert him'.[1] In *Émile* Rousseau had attacked rules of thumb. Émile was to learn nothing parrot-fashion, and to accept nothing purely on the word of authority; all his beliefs were to be fully integrated. But the political system advocated in *The Social Contract* was not, Godwin believed, consistent with this ideal. Godwin refers explicitly here to what Rousseau had said about the Legislator; but we have already seen that he was hostile to the whole concept of the general will, for much the same reason. He is almost certainly glancing at Rousseau when he speaks, in the chapter on national assemblies, of 'the absurdity of that fiction, by which society is considered, as it has been termed, a moral individual. . . . A multitude of men, after all our ingenuity, will still remain a multitude of men'.[2]

Godwin repeats this sentiment, in almost the same words, in the chapter on 'the political superintendence of opinion'. 'A multitude of men may be feigned to be an individual, but

[1] *P.J.* ii. 130.   [2] Ibid. 205.

they cannot become a real individual.'[1] In this chapter he deals with a good many of the institutions that Montesquieu had thought especially suited to the spirit of a republic: sumptuary and agrarian laws, as well as censorship and the prohibition of dangerous thoughts. We need not repeat his arguments against them, which are by now well-worn; but I think we may take it that he had Montesquieu's republic at least partly in mind when objecting both to paternalism in general and to the doctrine of the State as a super-individual in particular. His fundamental objection to all such doctrines is that they make it a virtue for the individual to sink his own judgement in the collective wisdom of the community. This is the way that prejudices are created; this is the root cause of the mental muddle that makes it possible for men who are not really cruel and unjust to behave cruelly and unjustly. Admittedly this acquiescence is necessary to all government; but that only means that government, as such, is bound to corrupt. And this indeed is what Godwin means when he says that government corrupts. It is not that rulers are wicked men who bend their subjects to their evil designs; it is that all of us, rulers and ruled alike, are bound to follow rules of thumb that make it impossible for any of us to see clearly what we are doing. War provides us with the most glaring example of this; but the case is not really different with the juryman who helps to send a poor wretch to prison or indeed with all of us in most of our daily concerns.

[1] *P.J.* ii. 217.

6

THE EMPIRE OF PREJUDICE

I

GODWIN's objection to both monarchy and republic can be put quite simply. Both of these forms of government create prejudice instead of curing it. They do this by inventing fictions: the nation, or the honour of a social class. These concepts act, as it were, as spectacles through which we see the world; and they are distorting spectacles.

The conclusion would seem to be plain: smash all the spectacles and look at the world with the naked eye of truth. And, since governments are (at least indirectly) responsible for these distorting glasses, can we perhaps smash the spectacles by getting rid of government? At times Godwin talks in this vein. But if we look more closely at what he says about prejudice, we will find that he realized that the problem was not quite as simple as that.

For the truth is that spectacles, of one kind or another, are firmly glued to all our noses. '. . . every idea', says Godwin, 'that now offers itself to the mind, is modified by all the ideas that ever existed in it. It is this circumstance, that constitutes the insensible empire of prejudice: and causes every object, which is exhibited to a number of individuals, to assume as many forms in their mind, as there are individuals who view it.'[1]

It would seem, then, that we are corrupted by the mere process of living. We can never quite see things as they are; because the present impression is modified by preconceived ideas, the effect of past impressions. There is indeed a passage

[1] *P.J.* i. 414.

in *Fleetwood* that would support this interpretation of Godwin. The hero is describing his disgust with the scenery round Oxford:

Nature spoils us for relishing the beauties of nature. Formed as my mind had been, almost from infancy, to delight itself with the grand, the romantic, the pregnant, the surprising, and the stupendous, as they display themselves in North Wales, it is inconceivable with what contempt, what sensations of loathing, I looked upon the face of nature as it shows itself in Oxfordshire. All here was flat and tame and tedious. Wales was nature in the vigour and animation of youth: she sported in a thousand wild and admirable freaks; she displayed a master-hand; every stroke of her majestic pencil was clear, and bold and free. But in the country to which I had now removed, nature to my eye seemed to be in her dotage; if she attempted anything, it was the attempt of a driveller; she appeared like a toothless and palsied beldame, who calls upon her visitors to attend, who mumbles slowly a set of inarticulate and unintelligible sounds, and to whom it exceeds the force of human resolution to keep up the forms of civility. Why does the world we live in, thus teach us to despise the world?[1]

Here we have a kind of prejudice with which governments would seem to have little to do; and one which it would be difficult indeed to guard against. But of course not all experience is corrupting. The mass of experience which we bring to every new percept usually helps us to see more clearly rather than less. It is not always the child who is best able to see the Emperor's nakedness; and Godwin must mean, I think, that only some kinds of preconceived idea are distorting. In its place in the novel this passage is meant to give a pointer to Fleetwood's character: he is a romantic who is quite unable to come to terms with the world in which he finds himself. And in describing his romanticism Godwin gives us much more typical examples of prejudice. He does this by con-

[1] *Fleetwood*, i. 46–47.

trasting Fleetwood with another character, Sir Charles Gleed, who is a dull fellow, but a realist:

While he saw only those things in character and action which formed the substance of what was seen by every beholder, he was led astray by no prepossessions or partialities, and drew a great number of just conclusions from the indications before him. I on the contrary entered every scene with certain expectations, and with a little system of my own forming ready digested in my mind. If I repaired to Notre Dame at Paris to assist at the celebrations of the high mass solemnised on the eve of the Nativity, my thoughts were full of the wonderful efficacy which religion exercises over my species, and my memory stored with the sublime emotions which altars and crucifixes and tapers had excited in the souls of saints and martyrs. If I entered the walls of the British House of Commons, and waited to hear an important debate, the scenes of past ages revolved before the eyes of my fancy, and that parliament again filled the benches in which Pym and Hampden, and Falkland and Selden, and Cromwell and Vane sat together, to decide, perhaps for ever, on the civil and intellectual liberties of my country. These are only instances. But in reality scarcely any character of the smallest importance came before me, in whom by retrospect or anticipation, by association of pride, of instruction, or of honour, I did not make to myself a lively interest, and whom I did not involuntarily surround with an atmosphere of my own creating, which refracted the rays of light, and changed the appearances of the scene. These causes rendered me a less dispassionate and therefore in many instances a less exact, though a much more earnest observer, than Sir Charles Gleed.[1]

All this is to explain how Fleetwood came to fall in love with a worthless woman. He offers these reflections indeed as a substitute for a detailed account of their affair:

I might delineate the ravishing sweetness of the weather on the day which first gave me possession of her person, the delightful excursion we made on the water, the elegantly furnished cottage

[1] *Fleetwood*, i. 142–4.

that received us, the very room, with all its furniture, which witnessed the consummation of my joys. All these things live in my memory. . . . But I suppress these circumstances, at the risk of rendering my narrative flat and repulsive by its generalities. I write no book that shall tend to nourish the pruriency of the debauched, or that shall excite one painful emotion, one instant of debate in the bosom of the virtuous and chaste.[1]

One feels sorry for those readers who bought Godwin's novels because of his reputation as a shameless advocate of free love. But the point to notice is that Sir Charles Gleed is not to be taken as, in general, a man who sees things as they are: for he is a debauchee, and an evil influence on Fleetwood. It was not at all Godwin's ideal to see only those things which are seen by every beholder. The Sir Charleses are led astray by their own prejudices; the point is simply that the delusions to which they are liable are of a different kind. This is confirmed by a passage in which Fleetwood is compared to a poet, and Sir Charles to a farmer, both looking at the Welsh mountains.

The poet . . . saw much less, though his mind was more active and at work than that of the farmer. The farmer's were perceptions; his were feelings. He saw things in masses, not in detail. He annexed a little romance to each. . . . It was not green and blue, ripe and immature, fertile and barren, that he saw; it was beauty and harmony and life, accompanied with a silent eloquence which spoke to his soul. . . . To express the difference in one word; what the farmer saw was external and in the things themselves; what the poet saw was the growth and painting of his own mind.[2]

It is easy to take this as a denunciation of all feeling. But Godwin would not, I think, deny that the poet sees much of value that is hidden from the farmer. And it is a fault in Sir Charles that he is deficient in feeling. 'Moral reasoning is nothing but the awakening of certain feelings'; but this does

[1] *Fleetwood*, i. 126.   [2] Ibid. i. 141–2.

not alter the fact that emotion in general is peculiarly liable to blind us to things as they are: to make us confuse 'the growth and painting of our own mind' with reality. As we have seen, the emotion of honour and the emotion of patriotism both do this. Fleetwood tells us how the process works: 'by associations of pride, of instruction, or of honour'. The operative word here is 'associations'. Fleetwood does not ask himself just what he admires in Pym and Hampden and the rest, and how far the members of the present House of Commons resemble them: he merely includes them all in one wave of feeling, and thereafter interprets the words and actions of the present members so as to make them worthy of that feeling. Godwin is not objecting to Fleetwood's admiration for Pym and Hampden: he is merely objecting to the uncritical extension of that feeling to those who are only associated with them in his mind, and not really like them in the respects that make them admirable. It is precisely this kind of extension that concepts like honour or patriotism encourage. They lead to an uncritical enthusiasm for everything connected, however remotely or accidentally, with the nobility or with our country. Consequently they fail, even as devices to make the nobles or the citizens themselves live up to the high traditions of their class or country; for there is a general fuzziness about precisely what it is that is to be emulated. We are only too likely to pride ourselves on all the worst features of the tradition.

Godwin seems indeed to have wavered in his condemnation of association. This is the result, I think, of his anxiety to admit the importance of the emotions, together with his distrust of abstraction and his belief that true knowledge is always knowledge of particulars, of an individual thing or person. You do not understand a generalization unless you see how it applies to a particular instance. Now it is significant that we use the word 'see' here; for in perception we do seem to have full and immediate knowledge: knowledge, moreover, that induces emotion as nothing else can. At one and the same time the spectators of Hume's shipwreck feel pity for the sailors and understand why their plight is pitiable; and it is not easy to distinguish between the two.

Now it is tempting to put this by saying that 'knowledge by description' needs to be supplemented by (or interpreted in the light of) 'knowledge by acquaintance', and that, when it is, 'mere reason' will be reinforced by emotion. Thus we find Godwin saying, in his *Life of Chaucer*,

It is the peculiar characteristic, I may add the peculiar beauty, of the Romish religion, that it so forcibly addresses itself to our senses, without losing sight of the immense advantage for giving permanence to a system of religion, which is possessed by creeds, dogmas, and articles of faith. Religion is nothing, if it be not a sentiment and a feeling. What rests only in opinion and specula-tion, may be jargon, or may be philosophy, but can be neither piety toward God nor love to man.[1]

If it stood by itself, we might interpret the appeal to the senses spoken of in this passage as the understanding of a generalization through acquaintance with an instance of it. But it is clear from what follows that this will not do. For Godwin goes on:

This truth was never more strikingly illustrated than in the history of the crusades. A man may be persuaded, by reading Grotius's treatise of the Truth of the Christian Religion, or any other work of a similar nature, that the man Jesus was really put to death eighteen hundred years ago, and that, after having been committed to the grave, he was seen again a living man; yet this persuasion may produce no effect upon his temper and his heart. Far different was the case, when the crusaders, after all their toils, and a difficult and obstinate siege, made themselves masters of Jerusalem by assault. They rushed toward the scene of the agony and death of their Saviour. They traced the venerable ground

[1] W. Godwin, *Life of Chaucer* (London, 1803), i. 43–44.

which had been hallowed by the tread of his feet. They saw the hill on which he died, the fragments of his cross, the drops still fresh and visible of his sacred blood. . . . Every one felt himself at this hour become a different man, and that a new spirit had taken its abode in his bosom.[1]

On the face of it, this looks much more like association than like the apprehension of an imperfectly understood generalization through acquaintance with one of its instances. The sights the crusaders saw were not instances of the dogma they came to believe more intensely. And if it is objected that historic scenes do help us to reconstruct past happenings, and so to understand them better, it may be pointed out that Godwin goes on to give other examples to which this argument does not apply. He speaks of the magnificence of Roman Catholic churches, 'the uniform garb of the monks and nuns . . . the splendour of the altar, the brilliancy of the tapers, the smoke and fragrance of the incense'. Wycliffe, he suggests, underestimated the importance of these aids to religious feeling:

Wicliffe was too nearly what has since been understood by the term, a puritan. He did not sufficiently take into account some of the fundamental properties of the human mind. He did not enough regard man as the creature of his senses. He was too severely inclined to strip religion of its ornaments. Enthusiasm, founded upon abstractions alone, is a short-lived passion. It may be lively and operative in one generation, but it will subside into torpor in the next. In the ordinary and transient concerns of human life we rarely feel a strong and permanent attachment but to what we see. In like manner in religion we can never have a system, uniform, genial and nutritive of the purest affections and habits, without the solemnities of worship, the decencies of architecture, the friendly alliance of harmonious sounds, or the fragrance of delicious odours.[2]

[1] Ibid., p. 44. [2] *Life of Geoffrey Chaucer*, ii. 217.

Now this is really a staggering paragraph to find in Godwin. That 'we rarely feel a strong and permanent attachment but to what we see' was one of his dearest beliefs. It was because of it that he wanted a small community in which each member could know his neighbour intimately. It was because of it that he distrusted 'abstractions', generalizations that could not be tested by concrete instances. He had insisted that right emotions, true opinions about what is good, arise from acquaintance with individuals, from knowledge, not of generalizations, but of the particulars which they embody. And now, it seems, he is prepared to extend this principle to include any emotion engendered by association, provided only that the association is with a sensory percept; so that Fleetwood's uncritical reverence for the House of Commons, or for the ceremony at Notre Dame, is all right after all. This is surely a complete reversal of all that he had said about reason.

But Godwin was a voluminous writer, and a hasty one. As he himself noted, he was often led away by his own eloquence until he said more than he meant. All he really wants to do here, I think, is to point to a psychological peculiarity of human beings. It is a fact that the senses have this kind of 'influence over the heart and character',[1] and it is folly to ignore that fact. Moreover, we will never 'have a system uniform, genial and nutritive of the purest affections and habits' if we do ignore it. But that is not to say that these emotions can never lead us astray, or that they should not be corrected by reason. Wycliffe's fault was not so much that he was wrong, but that he was before his time:

With the unenlightened and unthinking part of mankind, the whole circle of moral principles is bound together. They are fastened upon them by education, and confirmed by habit. Things sacred in themselves, are not sacred in their eyes from an intrinsic claim, but as connected with time and place, with outward

[1] *Life of Geoffrey Chaucer*, i. 44.

ceremonies and solemn observances. It is only a virtue founded in principle, and nurtured in the genial soil of a well ordered mind, that will survive unhurt, when the prejudices upon which it used to learn for support are no more. We may therefore reasonably conclude that Wicliffe and his partisans did much at least temporary mischief. They disturbed the visions and poetic forms of morality and religion.[1]

Associations of this kind are then, after all, a cause of prejudice. But prejudice must not be too rudely shattered. For it is also true that 'Religion is nothing, if it stop at a theoretical persuasion of the truth of certain propositions. It must become a vital principle, it must affect the heart and act upon the passions, before it can greatly modify the character of man in society.'[2] The proper way to make a principle 'act upon the passions' is to connect it, not with 'outward ceremonies and solemn observances', but with those concrete particulars that really constitute its meaning. There are two opposite errors which we must avoid: barren dogma, which does not really touch our 'hearts and characters', and principles which are indeed reinforced by emotion, but only because of quite adventitious associations. If we fall into either error, we hold a principle without really understanding it, and a principle so held is always a prejudice, whether it happens to be true or false. Godwin does seem inclined to add (at least when writing the *Life of Chaucer*) that, of the two kinds of error, the second may be preferable: to that extent he agrees (surprisingly) with Burke. But he is not, I think, saying more than that.

Godwin has a further account of the empire of prejudice: one that is not really different from this.

An individual surrenders the best attribute of man, the moment he resolves to adhere to certain fixed principles, for reasons not now present to his mind, but which formerly were. . . . There can be no scheme more egregiously stamped with folly, than that of

[1] Ibid. ii. 395.   [2] Ibid. 385.

separating a tenet from the evidence upon which its validity depends. If I cease from the habit of being able to recall this evidence, my belief is no longer a perception, but a prejudice: it may influence me like a prejudice; but cannot animate me like a real apprehension of truth.[1]

We have already seen what Godwin means by this, in his illustration of the habitual churchgoer.[2] The point at the moment is that the patriot, or the aristocrat, is in precisely this position, in so far as he is loyal to his country or his class just because it is his country or his class. This is quite different from admiring one's country for the qualities that make it admirable: which would involve admiring other countries with the same qualities, and also being ready to renounce those qualities which were not admirable.

We are now, I think, in a position to see what Godwin regards as the causes of prejudice. The most important of them is association: the illegitimate extension of some principle (X is to be admired, despised, reverenced, &c.) to something else, Y, which is like X in some respects, but not in the respects that make it admirable, despicable, &c. This is only possible when we have forgotten what those respects were; when, that is to say, we 'separate a tenet from the evidence on which its validity depends'.

But, of course, we may not have forgotten the evidence: we may never have known it. This is the second great cause of prejudice; and perhaps this is what is really wrong with both honour and 'virtue': we are never given any clear idea of what it is about our country or our class that demands our loyalty. This, as we have seen, is the main issue on which Godwin quarrels with Rousseau: when the minority acquiesces in a decision it inevitably accepts a tenet without knowing (in the full sense of 'know') the evidence on which it is based. This is a defect inherent in all government; and this is why govern-

[1] *P.J.*, ii. 299–300.   [2] See above, ch. 2, p. 54.

ment corrupts. This is also the objection to all forms of in-doctrination. It is also one of Godwin's main arguments against punishment, since to abstain from an action from fear of punishment is also to separate a principle from the evidence on which it is based.

These are the most general and far-reaching causes of pre-judice. But I think Godwin would say that there are four more which are very important. One is the lack of frankness which, as we have seen, is especially strong in any society based on prestige. This causes prejudice in a rather different way: it leads men to conceal the evidence on which principles should be based, and so tends to the formation of wrong principles. The second is the complexity of most modern communities, which makes it impossible to keep clearly in mind the evi-dence on which principles are based. This follows from God-win's conviction that human beings are unique, and any generalization about them only approximately true. I think he might say that they can be used safely only when the num-ber of instances to which they apply is so small that the differ-ences between each can be easily kept in mind. The mother who says: 'All my children are delicate' runs little risk of con-fusing John's chest trouble with Mary's weak stomach. She knows that the generalization is a shorthand way of referring to a number of quite different particulars, each of them unique. But we can easily forget this when we make generalizations about a nation or a social class, most of whose members we have not met and cannot meet. Generalizations of this kind are, then, bound to be inaccurate and can be fairly called prejudices.

The third cause of prejudice is the partiality we all have for a few friends and relations as against the rest of mankind. The fourth is the institution of punishment. Each of these will need to be discussed more fully.

We have already seen that the private and domestic

affections gave Godwin a lot of trouble. It is usual to say that he began by condemning them unreservedly, and then either withdrew hurriedly when he saw the fuss he had caused, or (if the critic is kinder) changed his mind after his own experience of domestic joy with Mary Wollstonecraft. But Godwin was never, in his private life, as cold as he is sometimes made out; and we do not need to look outside his theory itself to explain this conflict of attitude. Friendship is an obvious cause of prejudice: we find it entirely natural to say, when speaking of someone's opinion of a brother, parent or mistress: 'But of course he's prejudiced.' In elaborating a moral theory in which prejudice was made the source of all evil, Godwin was bound to be suspicious of private affection. But, on the other hand, to see human beings as they are is to see them intimately, at close quarters, in the way Hume's onlookers see the terror on the faces of the shipwrecked sailors. It is only our closest friends that we know in this way. It is not only that we are not likely to get close enough to people to know them thoroughly unless we are fond of them: unless we are fond of them we will not have the sympathy for them that is necessary to full understanding. This theme is stressed in all Godwin's novels, and especially in *St. Leon* and *Fleetwood*.

We have, then, this position. We cannot act rightly unless we know just why human beings behave as they do; and, since every individual is unique, we need to know this in detail of each individual. General principles will of course help us; but they can be misleading unless we fully realize that they are only approximations, or, as Godwin puts it, 'resting-places for the mind'. In the nature of things we can have this knowledge of only a few people; and only then if we are fond of them. Obviously we run a great risk of being unjust to the great mass of mankind whom we cannot know intimately. And there is a further reason why we are likely to be unjust to them. For, to be virtuous, we need knowledge of another kind as well; we need to grasp such principles as that 'we shall not give that exertion to procure the pleasure of an individual, which might have been employed in procuring the pleasure of many individuals'. We could not indeed help feeling this if we did have that vivid appreciation of the joys and sorrows of all mankind that we have of our handful of friends; but this is impossible. It would seem, then, that we can never know the principle of impartiality at all, in the full sense of 'know': it can never be more than a rule of thumb for us. Hume (though his approach is of course quite different from Godwin's) does indeed draw this conclusion: he says that, though disinterested benevolence does exist, it is always too restricted in its range to be a safe basis for social harmony; the legislator must, therefore, proceed as if self-interest were the sole human motive. Godwin resists this conclusion: he does not believe that there is any other safe basis for society, if universal benevolence is ruled out; but he does see the magnitude of the problem, and he is continually grappling with it. I do not know that he ever really solved it. We shall see in a moment how he tried to; but in the meantime we must consider the fourth cause of prejudice, the institution of punishment.

Godwin's views on punishment are a central part of his whole social theory. He devotes a whole book of *Political Justice* to this topic. I think that what he says is not altogether consistent; but the subject is peculiarly difficult and one that has never been satisfactorily dealt with. Godwin does put his finger on the central difficulty: our feelings about punishment depend on the concept of guilt, and guilt is a very slippery concept indeed. It is hard either to justify it or to dispense with it.

The principle of retribution is, Godwin says, included in the definition of punishment. Punishment is defined as 'the voluntary infliction of evil upon a vicious being, not merely because the public advantage demands it, but because there is apprehended to be a certain fitness and propriety in the nature of things, that render suffering, abstractedly from the benefit to result, the suitable concomitant to vice'.[1] Otherwise we would have to regard compulsory military service, or putting to death a man with a contagious disease, as punishment, since both these are examples of inflicting evil for the general bene-fit. But in fact, Godwin argues, it is absurd to suppose that punishment is justified if no good results either to the offender or to others.

This argument can be quite easily met by saying that punishment is justified only when two criteria are satisfied: there must be antecedent guilt as well as beneficial conse-quences. Godwin does not consider this obvious rejoinder; but it soon appears that he would not be prepared to accept the retribution principle even in this modified form. The reason, of course, is his determinism. 'The assassin cannot help the murder he commits, any more than the dagger.'[2] To say this is to dismiss the concept of guilt altogether. If any justification of punishment remains, it can only be the bene-ficial consequences, either to the offender or to society.

One would expect Godwin, then, to take his stand firmly on the utilitarian theory of punishment. One would expect him to say that the happiness of the individual may, on occasion, be sacrificed to the general happiness. The question of guilt or innocence does not then arise, unless it can be shown that the general happiness can never be served by punishing the innocent. And indeed he does say boldly: 'It is right that I should inflict suffering, in every case where it can be clearly shown that such infliction will produce an overbalance of good. But this infliction bears no reference to the mere inno-cence or guilt of the person upon whom it is made. An inno-cent man is the proper subject of it if it tend to good; a guilty

[1] *P.J.* ii. 323.   [2] Ibid. 324.

man is the proper subject of it under no other point of view.'[1]
But when he comes to examine the usual arguments in favour
of punishment, he seems to reject them less because they do
not show that punishment 'tends to good' than because they
violate the retributive principle. Reformative punishment is,
it is true, ruled out as useless, since punishment cannot reform. But punishment to deter the offender is condemned
because it is directed against a possible future crime, not
against an actual past one.

There is not more reason, in many cases at least, to apprehend
that the man who has once committed robbery, will commit it
again, than the man who has dissipated his property at the gaming-
table or who is accustomed to profess that, upon any emergency,
he will not scruple to have recourse to this expedient. . . . The sum
of the argument under this head is, that all punishment for the
sake of restraint is punishment upon suspicion, a species of
punishment the most abhorrent to reason, and arbitrary in its
application, that can be devised.[2]

Why is it abhorrent to reason? Godwin makes no attempt
to show that punishment on suspicion may not, at least sometimes, cause 'an overbalance of good'. He is really appealing
to the conviction we all have that it is unjust to punish on
mere suspicion, i.e. that it is unjust to punish a possibly innocent man. He begins by asserting, on utilitarian grounds, that
punishment can be justified only by looking to the future,
never to the past; then he points out that no one can properly
be called guilty of a crime not yet committed. But here, of
course, the retributive principle has come in at the back door;
and the utilitarian and the retributive accounts of punishment
have been simply muddled.

This becomes even more obvious in what he says about
punishment to deter others. 'It must surely be a very artificial

<hr />

[1] Ibid. 327.   [2] Ibid. 339–40.

and injudicious scheme for guiding the sentiments of man-kind, to fix upon an individual as a subject of torture or death, respecting whom this treatment has no direct fitness, merely that we may bid others look on, and derive instruction from his misery.'[1] The reference to 'direct fitness' here looks like a direct appeal to the retributive principle in the form in which Godwin himself has stated it: 'a certain fitness and propriety in the nature of things that render suffering the suitable con-comitant to vice'. It is true that he explains what he means by fitness here: the things that can 'make me a fit subject of pain' are 'either absolute desert, which is absurd, or mischief I may be expected to perpetrate, or lastly, a tendency in what you do, to produce my reformation'. But actually, as we have seen, Godwin has just denied that 'mischief I may be expected to perpetrate' really makes me a fit subject of pain; and he has ruled it out, not as he has ruled out reformation, because it is ineffective, but as simply unjust. This is certainly a muddle. What is even more glaring is that punishment for the sake of example is simply left out: Godwin disposes of it merely by omitting it from his list of valid reasons for punishing. He does not try to show that it is not effective, or that it can never cause more happiness to others than pain to the offender. Godwin is really appealing, once again, to the principle that it is never just to punish an innocent man. But, it may be objected, he is talking about guilty men, about those who have committed some crime. True, but he has two arguments to show that no one is ever really guilty. We have just seen what the first is. To show its inconsistency, it may be stated thus: punishment is always justified by reference to its effects, and not at all by reference to the past, i.e. to guilt or innocence. The crimes to be considered are therefore future crimes, those about to be committed either by the man to be punished or by someone else. But no one is ever guilty of crimes not yet

[1] *P.J.* ii. 346.

committed, and still less is he guilty of the crimes of others. Therefore deterrent punishment, whether for restraint or for example, is never just.

Godwin did not see the inconsistency here because he had always, at the back of his mind, another and much more cogent argument. Only the guilty should be punished; but no one is guilty if he could not help doing what he did; and in fact no one can help doing anything he does. This is, I think, a very large part of Godwin's objection to punishment. The difficulty is that the first premiss seems to be simply a datum, a self-evident principle. It is not obviously derived from the greatest happiness formula: indeed the greatest happiness formula leads Godwin to reject it. He must, therefore, look for other arguments; and in doing so he gets muddled.

It is possible, then, that on this matter Priestley is right, and Godwin is not really a utilitarian. But it is quite clear that Godwin himself did not realize this; and if pressed I think he might have abandoned the muddled arguments we have been discussing and said something like this. Punishment cannot be justified on retributive grounds, because the retributive first premise is inconsistent with determinism. It can therefore be justified, if at all, only on utilitarian grounds; but if we look more closely we find that, in the long run, punishment always causes more harm than good. The reason (and there can be no doubt that Godwin did believe this) is that it is one of the main causes of human prejudice. Which brings us back to our starting-point.

Punishment is doubly a cause of prejudice. First, it obscures the real reasons for doing right. 'Moral reasoning is nothing but the awakening of certain feelings'; and punishment awakens quite other feelings: certainly fear, and probably resentment as well. That is why punishment can never reform: it is much more likely to corrupt. In one of Godwin's later novels, *Cloudesley*, the hero robs a child of his inheritance.

He is led to do this because he has been hardened by a term in prison. He repents when he gets to know his innocent victim. Reform, that is to say, is not to be brought about by punishment but by coming to understand the real consequences of our actions: punishment merely substitutes an artificial set of consequences, and so obscures things as they are.

Secondly, the demands of punishment as an institution lead us to divide human actions into very rough and ready categories—lawyer's categories, which necessarily fail to do justice to the very complex behaviour of human beings. The hard and fast distinction which the law courts must make between the innocent and the guilty is itself difficult to justify, even if we disregard the connexion between guilt and free will. We may indeed, Godwin says, draw it with some exactness if we confine ourselves to external actions; though even then we must lump together much behaviour which is really quite different. Murder, for example, will be 'the exertion of any species of action affecting my neighbour, so as that the consequences terminate in death',[1] whatever the motive may have been. But the advocates of punishment themselves admit that guilt depends on motive; and any serious attempt to determine and classify motives would, Godwin says, soon make us realize 'how vain and presumptuous it is . . . to attempt to wield the rod of retribution'.[2] This is not merely because it is so difficult to determine motives that we seldom know even our own at all accurately; it is also because every human action is unique, and almost infinitely complex. The absurdity of law is 'the absurdity of bringing every offence to be compared with a certain number of measures previously invented, and compelling it to agree with one of them'.[2]

What a vast train of actual and possible motives enter into the history of a man, who has been incited to destroy the life of an-

[1] *P.J.* ii. 349.   [2] Ibid. 352.

other? Can you tell how much in these there was of apprehended justice, and how much of inordinate selfishness? How much of sudden passion, and how much of rooted depravity? How much of intolerable provocation, and how much of spontaneous wrong? How much of that sudden insanity which hurries the mind into a certain action by a sort of incontinence of nature, almost without any assignable motive, and how much of incurable habit? Consider the uncertainty of history. Do we not still dispute whether Cicero was more a vain than a virtuous man, whether the heroes of ancient Rome were impelled by vain glory or disinterested benevolence, whether Voltaire were the stain of his species, or their most generous and intrepid benefactor? Upon these subjects moderate men perpetually quote the impenetrableness of the human heart. Will moderate men pretend, that we have not an hundred times more evidence upon which to found our judgment in these cases, than in that of the man who was tried last week at the Old Bailey?[1]

'The fable of Procrustes', Godwin exclaims a little later, 'presents us with a faint shadow of the perpetual effort of law.'[2]

All this is, I believe, quite central to Godwin's thought. It explains, incidentally, why Godwin, whose talent was for pamphleteering and political speculation, should have spent so much of his time writing stilted fiction and pedestrian history. (Perhaps I should say, considering the context, that it tells us one of his motives: another was to earn his living.) Human beings are unique: we cannot hope to understand them unless we give to each individual the sympathetic understanding that a great novelist gives to his characters. Compare the magistrate's dressing-down of a prisoner with the story of his crime as it might be told by, let us say, Dostoievsky, and we can see what Godwin means. The magistrate writes contemporary history much in the spirit of *1066 and All That*; and, like the history taught in schools, the magistrate's categories, his good men and his bad men, his reputable

[1] *P.J.* ii. 353-4.   [2] *P.J.* ii. 403.

citizens and undesirable characters, his thieves, murderers, and prostitutes become stereotypes in the public mind. That is how stock attitudes grow up. Their inadequacy in helping us to understand human life as it is being lived all round us causes a very great part of human misery. That is what Godwin means by prejudice; and that is the way in which governments, through their institutions, and in particular the institution of punishment, may be held responsible for it.

But, it will at once be asked, can we in practice do without punishment? Godwin has to admit that we cannot, at least in society as we know it at present: and he never advocated sudden or violent change. Punishment, then, is justified as 'a temporary expedient'; but we should not punish in any spirit of righteous indignation. We have no right to do more than restrain men who seem certain to commit crimes if left at large; but we should regard the necessity as a painful one, and the victims as more to be pitied than censured. We should do what we can to reform them while they are in prison; while recognizing (and here Godwin is more clear-sighted than many prison reformers) that imprisonment is in itself an obstacle to reform. Godwin's practical conclusions about punishment (if we disregard a somewhat Utopian scheme for a penal colony in which the convicts were to be left completely to themselves) are not very different from those of a good many thoughtful and humane men today. The chief theoretical difficulty about them is that, in refusing to recognize that the distinction between guilt and innocence has any final validity, they seem to open the way to 'restraining' (in a spirit of pity and regret) men who have committed no crime, but who may, for one reason or another, be thought of as public enemies. Godwin would, of course, have been horrified at the suggestion; but it would seem to follow from his principles all the same. It seems that we cannot, after all, dispense with the principle that only antecedent guilt justifies punishment; though we may readily concede that it is not justified even then unless the punishment seems likely to prevent further crimes. But it is true enough that our notions of guilt are rough and ready, and that a complete understanding of the crime might lead us to pity the criminal instead of blaming him. Shall we, then, abolish punishment altogether? Certainly, if we can; but if we can't (and it is after all a little disingenuous to talk of 'temporary expedients' when you admit, as Godwin did, that any change might take centuries) what then? Shall we at least abolish all the cant about guilt and admit that we punish for reasons of expediency only? Why not, then, if expediency demands it, punish the innocent? We can see why Godwin keeps on reintroducing the retributive principle after he has formally banished it. But it is one thing to point out his inconsistency, and quite another to solve his problem.

2

If these are the causes of prejudice, what is its cure? Or, putting the question another way, what does Godwin propose to put in the place of monarchy and republic, since he has rejected both of them? What kind of society will remove the causes of prejudice? We can answer this question only by considering them again one by one.

The first cause of prejudice is association, in the sense in which that is opposed to reason. Association operates, it will be remembered, chiefly in two ways: in the formation of sentiments, and of habits. An example of a sentiment is Fleetwood's tendency to transfer his feelings about saints and martyrs to religious institutions in general, or his feelings about Pym and Hampden to parliamentary institutions in general. An example of a habit is provided by the churchgoer in *Political Justice*, whom we discussed in Chapter 2. The point about habit, Godwin tells us, is that, though 'it proceeds upon judgment, the reasons of that judgment are out of sight and forgotten'.[1]

Both sentiments and habits have a kind of logic behind them though it is usually a faulty logic. Fleetwood's feelings can be represented as an argument from analogy: Pym and Hampden are to be respected and admired; so, then, are their modern counterparts. The argument is effective only so long as it is not fully brought to consciousness; for then it would be obvious that the M.P.s he is watching are not the counterparts of Pym and Hampden in the respects that made those men admirable. The reasoning behind habits, as we have seen, usually includes premises which are not now present to the mind, though they once were; and often enough they, too, would be rejected if they were once again brought to consciousness. The cure for this kind of prejudice, then, is to bring these unformulated or forgotten motives to consciousness.

But what has government to do with all this? Habit and sentiment seem inseparable from human behaviour in any society. If they are the cause of error, and so of evil, then it would seem that evil is ineradicable. Godwin would answer, I imagine, that he is not opposed to habit and sentiment as such, but to their uncritical acceptance. Part of his case against governments is, as we have seen, that they rely on the kind of sentiment that cannot stand thoughtful criticism: patriotism, or respect for a privileged social class. These are sentiments like Fleetwood's; they depend on lumping together things that may be very different. Today's noble lord is invested, quite unreasoningly, with the qualities of his illustrious ancestor; today's sordid war for an ignoble object is confused with yesterday's heroic fight for freedom. (Godwin would probably have added that the ancestor was not really illustrious, and the fight not really heroic, even in the

[1] *P.J.* i. 67.

first place, but that is beside the present point.) Governments, then, while not wholly responsible for this kind of prejudice, may certainly be blamed for encouraging it. But this does not mean that we can get rid of it simply by abolishing government.

The solution, Godwin seems to think, lies in independence. He has here, I think, taken a hint from Rousseau's *Émile*. Rousseau had said: 'There is only one man who gets his own way—he who can get it single-handed; therefore freedom, not power, is the greatest good. That man is truly free who desires what he is able to perform, and does what he desires. This is my fundamental maxim.'[1] The emphasis here is on freedom and happiness; Rousseau is pointing out that kings are dependent on their ministers, and that ministers are compelled to pander to the prejudices of their subjects. But it may also be argued that the man who does things for himself is compelled to think for himself. He sees the results of his actions always in front of his eyes. If he does proceed by rule of thumb, at least he must test it and modify it constantly. And this point of view is developed in *Émile* also. Émile is to learn nothing parrot fashion. He is to be asked to accept no principles except those he forms for himself as the result of his own experience.

It was characteristic of Godwin that he was always liable to be carried away by enthusiasm for his own ideas. He noted this himself in his diary: 'I have, perhaps, never been without the possession of important views and forcible reasonings; but they have ever been mixed with absurd and precipitate judgments, of which subsequent consideration has made me profoundly ashamed.'[2] One of his most famous absurdities occurs in his chapter on co-operation, when he suggests that, in the happy future commonwealth, there will be no concerts,

[1] J. J. Rousseau, *Émile* (Everyman ed., London, 1933), p. 48.
[2] C. Kegan Paul, *William Godwin*, i. 295.

since musicians will not demean themselves by performing in groups, and no plays. But it is worth noticing the grounds on which Godwin objects to these performances.

Shall we have concerts of music? The miserable state of mechanism of the majority of the performers, is so conspicuous as to be, even at this day, a topic of mortification and ridicule. Will it not be practicable hereafter for one man to perform the whole? Shall we have theatrical exhibitions? This seems to include an absurd and vicious co-operation. It may be doubted, whether men will hereafter come forward in any mode, formally to repeat words and ideas that are not their own. It may be doubted, whether any musical performer will habitually execute the composition of others. . . . All formal repetition of other men's ideas, seems to be a scheme for imprisoning, for so long a time, the operations of our own mind.[1]

Co-operation, it is clear, is linked in Godwin's mind with routines of action and stereotypes of thought. It is when men work together on a task that they fall into a 'miserable state of mechanism', forgetting the reasons for what they do. It is when men work together as members of a large institution that they form sentiments of the kind he condemns. The independent craftsman is much less likely to forget the purpose of his actions or to deceive himself about the value of his own activities.

This type of prejudice, then, is most likely to be avoided in a community of independent craftsmen. They need not be entirely self-sufficient: in spite of his praise of the one-man band, Godwin does not rule out division of labour and the exchange of goods, provided the exchange does not take the form of barter. Each man should give his surplus to those who need them simply because they need them. The craftsmen, though independent, will not be solitary. They will meet together often, because society is pleasant, and the exchange

[1] *P.J.* ii. 504.

of ideas valuable, provided no one tries to impose his ideas on another, and everyone keeps on thinking for himself. They will be particularly zealous in exchanging ideas about each other's conduct and character. 'What could be more beneficial, than for each man to derive assistance for correcting and moulding his conduct, from the perspicacity of his neighbours?'[1]

Unlike most twentieth-century anarchists, Godwin does not combine his idealization of the independent craftsman with a hatred of machinery and a *mystique* of the soil. On the contrary, he welcomes the machine as 'the Helot of the future', which will remove the drudgery from labour and make it possible for one man to do the work of many single-handed. He could conceivably have been Mr. Toogood[2] in *Crotchet Castle*: 'the Co-operationist, who will have neither fighting nor praying, but wants to parcel out the world into squares like a chess-board, with a community on each, producing everything for one another, and a great steam-engine in the middle to serve them in common as tailor and hosier, kitchen and cook'. That close co-operation would be needed to make the machine does not seem to have occurred to him.

The cure for the first cause of prejudice is also, very largely, the cure for the second. If the independent craftsman is not likely to act from mere habit, forgetting the reasons for his actions, he is still less likely to form habits without ever understanding the reasons for them. But here government may be more directly to blame: for it is, as we have seen, the need to acquiesce in the decisions of others that is largely responsible for this kind of prejudice.

It is here, as we have seen, that Godwin differs most markedly from Rousseau. But it might be thought that he

[1] Ibid. i. 496.
[2] Generally (and, I suppose, rightly) taken to be Robert Owen, who was, of course, influenced by Godwin.

differs only from the Rousseau of *The Social Contract*, and that Godwin, in sketching his ideal society, is merely drawing the political inferences from the *Discourse on the Origin of Inequality* and the *Dialogues* that Rousseau, for some reason, failed to draw. We are not concerned here with the question of Rousseau's consistency; but it will be convenient at this point to consider how far Godwin was influenced by Rousseau's psychological theories.

Godwin's advocacy of independence and his objection to co-operation almost certainly derive from Rousseau; and his attack on Honour is not at all unlike Rousseau's condemnation of *amour-propre*. But, whereas Rousseau seems to think of *amour-propre* as the root of all evil, for Godwin it is merely one source of prejudice among others, and not even the most important source: it may indeed, in the right circumstances, work for good. And there is nothing in Godwin quite corresponding to Rousseau's distinction between *amour-propre* and *amour de soi*.

According to Rousseau, there is no particular reason why self-love as such should make men quarrelsome. A man in the state of nature will occasionally find other men getting in the way of his desires, but not always or even often. There is, then, no necessary opposition between *amour de soi* and the other instinct that Rousseau postulates, *pitié*. It is the growth of society that stifles *pitié*; and it does this in three ways. First, the complexity of society, and the need for co-operation, make it more likely that other men will get in the way of our desires. Secondly, society encourages us to compare ourselves with others, and this gives rise to *amour-propre*. Since the prosperity of others makes our own position seem less happy by contrast, *amour-propre*, unlike *amour de soi*, is directly opposed to *pitié*. Thirdly, as well as encouraging *amour-propre* directly, society also encourages it indirectly, by teaching men to reason.

... à mesure que l'esprit s'étend, s'exerce et s'éclaire, il prend plus d'activité, il embrasse plus d'objets, saisit plus de rapports, examine, compare; dans ces fréquentes comparaisons, il n'oublie ni lui-même, ni ses semblables, ni la place à laquelle il prétend parmi eux.... Aussi remarque-t-on généralement, en confirmation de cette théorie, que les gens d'esprit, et sur-tout les gens de lettres, sont de tous les hommes ceux qui ont une plus grande intensité d'amour-propre, les moins portés à aimer, les plus portés à haïr.[1]

And this may be compared with a well-known passage in the *Discourse on the Origin of Inequality*:

It is reason that engenders *amour-propre*, and reflection that confirms it: it is reason which turns man's mind back upon itself, and divides him from everything that could disturb or afflict him. It is philosophy that isolates him, and bids him say, at sight of the misfortunes of others: 'Perish if you will, I am secure.' Nothing but such general evils as threaten the whole community can disturb the tranquil sleep of the philosopher, or tear him from his bed. A murder may with impunity be committed under his window; he has only to put his hands to his ears and argue a little with himself, to prevent nature, which is shocked within him, from identifying itself with the unfortunate sufferer. Uncivilised man has not this admirable talent; and for want of reason and wisdom, is always foolishly ready to obey the first promptings of humanity. It is the populace that flocks together at riots and street-brawls, while the wise man prudently makes off. It is the mob and the market-women, who part the combatants, and hinder gentle-folk from cutting one another's throats.[2]

If Rousseau simply means that society does in fact inculcate prejudices that often stifle compassion, Godwin would

---

[1] Second Dialogue, *Œuvres de J. J. Rousseau* (Paris, Werdet et Lequien Fils, 1826), xvi. 231.
[2] *The Social Contract* and *Discourses* (Everyman ed., tr. G. D. H. Cole, London, 1920), p. 199. I have kept the word used by Rousseau, *amour-propre*.

no doubt agree with him; but he seems to mean more than this. He seems to suggest that 'reason', since it consists in making comparisons, leads quite inevitably to *amour-propre*. Reason is thus opposed to sensibility, which gives *pitié* a chance to manifest itself. Now Godwin, although he agrees that men feel compassion when they see 'things as they are', does not regard reason as an obstacle to seeing things as they are. It is true that we may, by classifying, abstracting and comparing, lose sight of the individual altogether; and this is, as we have seen, one source of prejudice. Nevertheless, it is only through reason that we can attain to a knowledge of things as they are: Godwin does not think that Rousseau's savage, or even his market-woman, is likely to have this knowledge. What is needed is a quite subtle insight into the motives of other men, and some appreciation of the way in which they have come to be what they are. We shall never attain this insight without sympathy; but sympathy by itself is not enough to give it to us. And Godwin would certainly have said that the cult of sensibility had its own dangers.

He may, indeed, have had Rousseau partly in mind when, in *Fleetwood*, he portrayed 'the new man of feeling'. Rousseau is mentioned by name more than once in that novel; and Fleetwood is not at all unlike the self-portrait Rousseau gives us in the *Dialogues*. Each of these heroes of fiction (for it is hard to think of Rousseau's 'Jean-Jacques' as anything else) spent his youth seeking the ideal figures his imagination had created; each thought, on slight evidence, that he had found them; each, in his subsequent disillusionment, turned away from the world and took refuge in solitude.[1] But, whereas Rousseau speaks of Jean-Jacques as *l'homme naturel*, Godwin makes it clear that Fleetwood is merely an awful example. He needs more sense and less sensibility:

[1] Second Dialogue, *Œuvres de J. J. Rousseau* (Paris, 1826), xvi. 253 et seq.

he lacks the robust sense of reality that reason might have given him.

Further, Godwin would not, I think, agree with Rousseau that *amour de soi* is relatively harmless because, in a state of nature, it is limited. Natural man, according to Rousseau, pursues his own advantage when he sees it under his nose: with equal directness he flies to the help of others when moved by *pitié*. It is only when civilized that he learns to pursue his more remote advantage, and it is this remote advantage that comes into conflict with *pitié*; prompting him, for example, 'to put his hands over his ears and argue with himself' when murder is being committed under his window. Godwin's psychology owes much more to Hartley. Self-interest leads us, through the mechanism of association, to widen the range of our pleasures until we quite spontaneously identify ourselves with others. It is true that Godwin rejects the view that sympathy is merely a more refined form of self-interest; but he still wants to say that the more we reason, even about self-interest, the closer we come to sympathy. Self-love and sympathy are not warring instincts each of which is to be kept within its own proper sphere. If we really think about our own pleasure, we cannot help coming to feel that what is desirable for us is also desirable for other people. We may think of this as an axiom of reason coming in to correct self-interest; or we may prefer to say that, as we come nearer to knowing other people as well as we know ourselves, we feel the same urgent desire for their welfare that we have for our own. On this second view, reason has the job of increasing our knowledge of other people. Godwin, as we have seen, wavered between these points of view; but, whichever he adopts, he differs from Rousseau. The application of reason to self-interest (provided that it really is reason, and not prejudice) does not stifle compassion, but awakens it.

The other causes of prejudice we enumerated were lack of

frankness, the complexity of society, the domestic affections, and the institution of punishment. Lack of frankness is less likely, Godwin thinks, in a society with no artificial distinctions of rank or prestige. Insincerity is caused, partly by the need of the poor to flatter the rich and the need of the rich to impress the poor, and partly by the need of everybody to keep up with the Joneses. There will be no need for any of this in the classless society. Godwin would, I think, have agreed with Bernard Shaw that the penalty of hypocrisy is not so much being found out as having to live up to the role one has assumed.[1] Men will be thankful enough to be themselves once there is no social penalty attached. But it is hard to see frankness resulting from Godwin's happy band of brothers eagerly examining each other's faults.

The complexity of society is of course to be overcome by keeping our model communities small. The tiny state was part of the republican ideal, largely in order to make it possible for all the citizens to meet and vote in the legislative assembly. Godwin did not want them to meet and vote; but if every citizen is to go his own way without being bound by any set rules, the community must be even smaller.

What is to be done about the domestic affections? Godwin does not want to eliminate them: the problem is rather to extend them until they embrace everybody. But this is impossible. Perhaps this is another reason for keeping the community very small: Godwin's ideal society does, indeed, seem to be something like an extended family group, though one in which the individual members have unusual independence and privacy. In the first edition of *Political Justice* he thought that it might be an advantage if the men in his ideal community did not know which of the children they had fathered; and surnames, he suggested, would be abolished. All this is reminiscent of Plato; but these specula-

[1] See Godwin, W., *Deloraine* (London, 1833), v. 3, p. 267–71.

tions did not survive reflection. His more considered opinion is that marriage in the ideal state will be not very unlike marriage now; except that divorce will be easy, though not necessarily frequent, there will be less fuss over occasional infidelity (which is still not to be encouraged), and an end to the romantic, love-at-first-sight, world-well-lost tradition that causes so much self-deception and unhappiness. Godwin on marriage, so shocking to his contemporaries, reads today like a mild and rather priggish reformer of the nineteen-twenties.

Godwin's indictment of the romantic attitude to marriage is significant.

The method is, for a thoughtless and romantic youth of each sex, to come together, to see each other, for a few times, and under circumstances full of delusion, and then to vow eternal attachment. What is the consequence of this? In almost every instance they find themselves deceived. They are reduced to make the best of an irretrievable mistake. They are led to conceive it their wisest policy, to shut their eyes upon realities, happy, if, by any perversion of intellect, they can persuade themselves that they were right in their first crude opinion of each other. Thus the institution of marriage is made a system of fraud; and men who carefully mislead their judgments in the daily affair of their life, must expect to have a crippled judgment in every other concern.[1]

Fleisher thinks it odd that Godwin should find self-deception the chief evil here, rather than 'the fact that these young people are condemned to life-long unhappiness'.[2] But this is quite consistent with Godwin's views on prejudice in general. The source of all evil is an inability to see things as they are. To shut one's eyes to the defects of one's family, or friends, or class, or nation may seem an amiable weakness; but an elaborate superstructure of falsehood may well rise on such a

[1] *P.J.* ii. 507.
[2] David Fleisher, *William Godwin* (London, 1951), p. 102.

foundation. Mark Twain thought that Sir Walter Scott was directly responsible for the American Civil War: the feudal ideals of chivalry and honour, admirable enough in themselves, made the southerners quite incapable of understanding the world in which they were living. Godwin would have seen this as confirmation, not merely of his criticism of the ideal of 'honour', but of his general thesis about prejudice. For him self-deception is always the worst of evils.

His basic objection to the domestic affections, then, is that they lead us to nurse illusions about our friends and families. But we have already seen that there is a problem here that goes to the heart of Godwin's philosophy. For Godwin also believes that we cannot hope to see any individual as he really is unless we are very close to him and observe him with the utmost sympathy: we must always remember that every human being is unique, and extremely complex. If we do see a man as he really is, we can hardly help wishing him well; but since we can, in the nature of things, know only a few individuals intimately, it would seem that Hume is right and that benevolence must always be restricted: too restricted to be a safe basis for society.

I am not sure that Godwin ever really solved this problem. I do not know, indeed, that he ever saw it in quite this form; though it is obvious that he was perplexed by the whole question of the domestic affections, and I think that this was the real cause of his perplexity. But I think we can see, in general terms, how he tried to escape from this dilemma. We need to notice, first of all, that there is an apparent inconsistency in what I have said. The domestic affections lead us to nurse illusions about our friends and families; but we are bound to nurse illusions about everyone we do not know intimately, i.e. about everyone except our friends and families. If Godwin believes both these things, he must obviously distinguish between two possible attitudes to our intimates.

Affection may be based on self-deception; but it may also be based on an unusually thorough clearness of sight and depth of understanding. It is one thing to pardon everything because we understand everything: quite another to pardon everything because we stubbornly refuse, in the teeth of all the evidence, to believe that there is anything to pardon. It is only the second of these that Godwin condemns; and it is only the second that, by leading us on to further distortions of fact in order to prevent ourselves from detecting the original one, makes us finally unfit to understand and cope with the world around us. The first attitude, on the other hand, increases our understanding of human behaviour and makes us better able to cope with it.

There is, then, an essential difference between partiality and benevolence. However we may rationalize it, partiality consists essentially in making exceptions in favour of ourselves or our friends. Self-deception is necessary just because we do feel impelled to rationalize the process. But making exceptions in favour of individuals obviously cannot be extended to all men: this would be inherently contradictory. And the rationalizations into which partiality leads us are those which make us unjust to other men; we may, for example, be led into theories about Aryan superiority or about 'natural slaves'. But the benevolence that is based on understanding may, at least in principle, be extended to all men; and if, on the basis of our intimate understanding of our friends, we are led to generalize about other men, the generalizations have at least some chance of being true. All Godwin's fluctuations of opinion about the domestic affections may, I think, be reduced to two propositions. Partiality is the great enemy to universal benevolence; friendship is the only possible basis for it. In the first edition of *Political Justice* he was struck by the importance of the first proposition; in his emendations and in the novels he tried to redress the balance by emphasizing the second; but there is no real inconsistency.

Nevertheless, he has not quite solved his problem. He wants to say that the only way to become virtuous is to see things as they are; once we know the facts we cannot but feel the appropriate emotions towards those facts. If we really know another human being, we cannot but feel sympathy and good feeling for him, and these are the appropriate emotions. But it is a basic axiom of morals that these emotions are appropriate to all men. If we cannot actually feel them towards all men, we should at least behave as if we did. But we cannot hope to know all men intimately. We cannot, then, know the full facts on which this fundamental moral principle is based: it must then remain a rule of thumb for us. But, if it is a rule of thumb, how can Godwin be so certain that it is true, since he seems to think that rules of thumb are almost invariably false? But perhaps this is not quite fair: the point about rules of thumb is not so much that they are false as that we are likely to go astray in applying them to any particular instance. This would merely mean that men are bound to be wavering and uncertain in their morality. Godwin would have no difficulty about admitting that they are wavering and uncertain, but can he say that they are bound to be? This would seem to mean abandoning the doctrine of human perfectibility.

Perhaps, however, he would not think so.

By perfectible [he is careful to tell us] it is not meant that he is capable of being brought to perfection. But the word seems sufficiently adapted to express the faculty of being continuously made better and receiving perpetual improvement; and in this sense it is here to be understood. The term perfectible, thus explained, not only does not imply the capacity of being brought to perfection, but stands in express opposition to it. If we could arrive at perfection, there would be an end to our improvement.[1]

[1] *P.J.* i. 93.

He is even prepared to grant that there may be 'something in the nature of man incompatible with absolute perfection', and that the notion of perfection may itself be 'pregnant with absurdity and contradiction'. Moreover, he is inclined to think that the reason for this has something to do with 'the limited nature of the human faculties'. 'We can neither be present to all places nor to all times.' Man is 'a being shut in on all sides'. Godwin might, then, have been prepared to accept the conclusion that men can never be fully seized of the principle of universal benevolence, simply because they cannot hope to know all their fellows intimately. On the other hand, he also says, in the same passage, that perfectibility implies that 'every perfection or excellence that human beings are competent to conceive, human beings, unless in cases that are palpably and unequivocally excluded by the structure of their frame, are competent to attain. . . . Every principle which can be brought home to the conviction of the mind, will infallibly produce a correspondent effect on the conduct.' But it is still open to him to say that universal benevolence is something we cannot really 'conceive', or be, in the full sense, convinced by. And perhaps he does mean no more than that this is an ideal towards which we can strive, and which, if it can never be reached, can always be brought a little closer. It is certainly always possible to widen the area of our sympathies. At least we can remove some of the more obvious barriers between men. In the ideal community this is to be done by abolishing class distinctions, and by limiting the size of the community so that everyone will at least have some chance of knowing his neighbours intimately.

In such a community it might ultimately be possible, Godwin thought, to dispense with punishment, our sixth and last cause of prejudice. At least a small community would be more likely to avoid the more flagrant kinds of injustice. Any offender would be brought before a jury of his neighbours.

They would know him intimately, and so would judge him as an individual. To them he would be simply Old So-and-so, with this or that understandable human weakness, which was making him a nuisance. They would simply be friends conferring about the best way of helping a common friend and protecting themselves against his aberrations. This is quite different from what happens in our own society, where prisoner and magistrate often belong to different social worlds, and each must seem quite incomprehensible to the other. The jury, if compelled to punish at all, would at least be unlikely to do more than was absolutely necessary to restrain the offender. The prisoner on his side would have some chance of realizing just why his behaviour was obnoxious to his neighbours. Eventually, Godwin thought, punishment of any kind might become unnecessary.

It might then be sufficient for them to invite offenders to forsake their errors. If their expostulations proved, in a few instances, ineffectual, the evils arising out of this circumstance, would be of less importance, than those which proceed from the perpetual violation of the exercise of private judgment. But, in reality, no evils would arise: for, where the empire of reason was so universally acknowledged, the offender would either readily yield to the expostulations of authority: or, if he resisted, though suffering no personal molestation, he would feel so uneasy, under the unequivocal disapprobation, and observant eye, of public judgment, as willingly to remove to a society more congenial to his errors.[1]

It is difficult to take all this very seriously. One wonders how seriously Godwin himself took it. The main outlines of his ideal state are clear enough; but the details are left completely vague. We are told nothing, for example, of its economics except that there will be some division of labour and complete equality of income. This is usually taken to show what an unpractical dreamer Godwin was; but it is fairer to

[1] *P.J.* ii. 211.

say, I think, that he was not really a political reformer in the ordinary sense. He is not very interested in blueprints for a brave new world; he does not believe in political organizations, and he has no programme. He is primarily a moralist. He is chiefly concerned to analyse the causes of prejudice; once we understand these the cure may very well be left to look after itself. For all his brave talk of progress he makes it quite clear that his ideal state is set in the extremely remote future. We need to have some vague idea of the direction in which we wish to move; but we need have no more than that, because change can be brought about only very slowly and gradually. He insists again and again on the folly of violent change:

If the government of Great Britain were dissolved tomorrrow, unless that dissolution were the result of consistent and digested views of political truth previously disseminated among the inhabitants, it would be very far from leading to the abolition of violence. Individuals, freed from the terrors by which they had been accustomed to be restrained, and not yet placed under the happier and more rational restraint of public inspection, or convinced of the wisdom of reciprocal forbearance, would break out into acts of injustice, while other individuals, who desired only that this irregularity should cease, would find themselves obliged to associate for its forcible suppression. We should have all the evils and compulsory restraint attached to a regular government, at the same time that we were deprived of that tranquillity and leisure which are its only advantages.[1]

And again:

If, by positive institution, the property of every man were equalised to-day, without a contemporary change in men's dispositions and sentiments, it would become unequal to-morrow. The same evils would spring up with a rapid growth; and we should have gained nothing by a project which, while it violated

[1] *P.J.* ii. 366–7.

every man's habits, and many men's inclinations, would render thousands miserable.[1]

And yet again:

Evils often exist in a community, which, though mere excrescences at first, at length become so incorporated with the principle of social existence, that they cannot suddenly be separated, without the risk of involving the most dreadful calamities. . . . (We would not be justified in) the abrupt reduction of thousands to a condition, the reverse of that to which they had hitherto been accustomed, a condition, perhaps the most auspicious to human talent and felicity, but for which habit had wholly unfitted them, and which would be to them a continual source of dejection and suffering. It may be doubted, whether the genuine cause of reform, ever demands, that, in its name, we should sentence whole classes of men to wretchedness.[2]

Finally, Godwin speaks very unfavourably of the lawlessness of pre-feudal England: 'The barbarism of these times it is difficult for us without a violent stretch of fancy to conceive. There was no public law; or the voice of public law was unheard and ineffectual. There was no magistracy; or the magistrate possessed no power to bring the offender before him, and to inforce his decisions.'[3] It is obvious that he does not defend anarchy as such, without the attitudes of mind that are necessary to make it work.

It is worth emphasizing the frequency of these warnings, because it is obvious that to a man with these views detailed blueprints for the future are a waste of time. We can do nothing here and now but try to make a few small breaches in the wall of prejudice. If enough people can be brought to see what is wrong with society, society will right itself; but only by slow and gradual changes that will take generations. We cannot know in detail just what form the changes will

[1] *P.J.* ii. 438.   [2] Ibid. 448–9.
[3] *Life of Chaucer* (London, 1803), i. 27.

take; in the nature of the case only vague outlines are possible. There is no question of a political programme: political organizations are themselves a cause of prejudice. We are not even, as twentieth-century anarchists generally suggest, to point the way to the new society by setting an example of a better way of life. In the preface to *Fleetwood* Godwin is emphatic about this:

A thousand things might be found excellent and salutary, if brought into general practice, which would in some cases appear ridiculous, and in others be attended with tragic consequences, if prematurely acted upon by a solitary individual. The author of *Political Justice*, as appears again and again in the pages of that work, is the last man in the world to recommend a pitiful attempt, by scattered examples, to renovate the face of society, instead of endeavouring by discussion and reasoning to effect a grand and comprehensive improvement in the sentiments of its members.[1]

In our reasoning and discussion we will be concerned to break down existing prejudice. The immediate task is to destroy the current ideals of Honour or Virtue. These ideologies have been created by existing institutions; but they can be destroyed without destroying these institutions, because, strong though prejudice is, it cannot entirely blind men to the facts. It is at least always possible to show them some part of the truth. Opinion can be changed only slowly, when supported by existing institutions; but it can be changed, and as it changes the institutions will be gradually transformed.

Political Justice is Utopian only in the sense that Plato's *Republic* or Rousseau's *Contrat Social* are Utopian. Its main purpose is to answer the theoretical question: what is justice? not to put forward a manifesto or a practicable programme. Godwin is not, of course, of the stature of Plato or Rousseau; but he cannot be dismissed as a mere visionary any more than they.

[1] *Fleetwood* (London, 1805), i. xii.

7

CRITICISM

I

In this chapter I want to say something in criticism of Godwin. In one way it is much too easy to criticize him. He was a fluent and rhetorical writer, and an enthusiastic hunter of wild geese. He could never resist darting down side lanes in pursuit of these philosophical game, and they led him into a good many morasses. Moreover, he was, in the seventeen-nineties, immensely fashionable. This is partly because, like most fashionable philosophers, he can be read at two levels; his ideas can easily be put superficially. But it is also because they are often really superficial.

Encouraged by these obvious faults, most of Godwin's critics have been content to dismiss him far too lightly. And, before proceeding to my own criticism of Godwin, I will try to show that the usual criticism of him is much too facile.

Put in its briefest form, the most common objection is that Godwin was absurdly optimistic about human nature. When we consider the way in which human beings actually behave, it seems absurd to suggest that they are 'naturally good'. Secondly (though this is, perhaps, really the same objection in a different form), Godwin relied far too much on the power of reason. 'A fatal flaw', says Mr. Fleisher, 'lies at the heart of Godwin's system—an exaggerated notion of the power of reason over human conduct, an inadequate appreciation of the primal, brute forces in human nature that oppose reason.'[1]

---

[1] David Fleisher, *William Godwin* (London, 1951), p. 146.

It is fashionable at the present moment to reject the whole concept of natural goodness and to revert to the earlier doctrine of original sin. The reason usually given is that Godwin and his contemporaries have been refuted by history. In the eighteenth and nineteenth centuries, it is said, men could easily believe in the inevitable march of progress. The growth of science, of industry, and of education had opened up new possibilities of material comfort and mental enlightenment: it was natural to suppose that these would be accompanied by a moral revolution as well. But we can no longer believe this. For men do today live in tolerable comfort, and they do know a good deal about their physical environment; but they do not treat each other better. On the contrary, the twentieth century has shown us new abysses of cruelty and evil.

Now nothing in all this really touches Godwin. No doubt he was influenced, in a general way, by the prevailing belief that man was on the march; he does put his proposals for human betterment in the form of a prophecy. And he did think that machinery could, if wisely used, help to make a golden age possible. But he certainly did not think that it was being wisely used in his own time, nor would he think that it has been wisely used since. He does occasionally talk encouragingly of the progress that mankind has made since primitive times; but he certainly did not think that progress would be quite automatic, and that each century would be better than the one before it. If Godwin were restored to life today, he might well regard the history of the twentieth century as confirming his central thesis, not as refuting it. The causes of prejudice were, he insisted, the complexity of civilization and the power of centralized authority. Civilization has become more complex and authority more powerful; it is not at all surprising that there have been new forms of evil.

It is usual to talk about Godwin's 'optimism'; but this can

be misleading. His writing often has a curiously hag-ridden
effect. Angus Wilson has detected this in his novels, and
finds it difficult to reconcile them with the mood of *Political
Justice*:

> There is a frightening chasm, a nightmare dissociation between
> the gloomy, tortured lives of Godwin's heroes and the sweet
> reasonableness, the universal good sense of *Political Justice*, though
> the horror of the novels gives full answer to the facile criticism of
> Godwin's anarchism on the grounds of psychological *naïveté* and
> failure to consider the problem of evil. It is true that the dicho-
> tomy is there, damaging both political treatise and romance, but
> Godwin was fully aware of this schizophrenic tendency.[1]

But is there any real 'dichotomy'? It is surely odd to
regard *Political Justice* as the work of a man who looks upon
the world and finds it good. 'The history of mankind', he
wrote in that book, 'is little else than a record of crimes. . . .
Though the evils that arise to us from the structure of the
material universe are neither trivial nor few, yet the history
of political society sufficiently shows that man is of all other
beings the most formidable enemy to man.'[2]

And again:

> Every animal, however minute, has a curious and subtle struc-
> ture, rendering him susceptible, as it should seem, of piercing
> anguish. We cannot move our foot, without becoming the means
> of destruction. . . . It may be said, with little licence of phraseology,
> that all nature suffers. . . . Let us view man, writhing under the
> pangs of disease, or the fiercer tortures that are stored up for him
> by his brethren. . . . The whole history of the human species,
> taken in one point of view, appears a vast abortion.[3]

Godwin's novels are little more than illustrations of such
passages as these. The history of our own times would only
have provided him with a further illustration. Godwin had

[1] Angus Wilson, 'The Novels of William Godwin', in *World Review*,
June 1951, p. 40.   [2] *P.J.* i. 6–7.   [3] Ibid. 455–7.

a very real, and possibly morbid, sense of the extent of man's inhumanity to man. His theory of natural goodness cannot be refuted by pointing to any number of instances of human cruelty, however bestial. Godwin had considered them all, only too thoroughly: and in saying that man is naturally good, he does not mean that man does not act evilly.

But perhaps this only opens the way to a more profound criticism. If the theory of natural goodness cannot be refuted by any appeal to the facts, by looking at man and seeing how he does actually behave, isn't it unverifiable and therefore meaningless? I have much more sympathy with this objection. But we must notice that it applies also to the opposing theory, about original sin. For this will not be refuted, either, by pointing to any number of instances of benevolence and heroism. To call man 'naturally' good or 'naturally' evil is indeed to say very little. The truth is that he sometimes behaves well and sometimes badly. The history of our own century, or of any other, will not really take us very far beyond that conclusion.

But of course this is not all that can be said. For Godwin's belief in natural goodness has nothing to do with the extent or the frequency of evil: it is a hypothesis about its causes. More accurately, it is the hypothesis that it has causes, and that we ought to look for them. To talk about original sin is to give up the search for the causes of sin. It is as if we were to say: 'Disease is a natural phenomenon', and turn our backs on medicine. Of course disease is a natural phenomenon; but that does not alter the fact that any given disease has an assignable cause, and that if we can find the cause we may be able to cure it. You do not in the least refute that assertion by pointing to the vast extent of disease, or even by showing that the modern advances that have enabled us to cure some diseases have caused others to multiply. Godwin is making the same assertion about human wickedness. In general, no doubt, it is always with us, like disease; but any particular piece of wickedness, like any particular disease, has specific causes, usually social ones; and it may be possible to remove them. That the causes are far-reaching and difficult to remove, Godwin did not deny.

Of course natural goodness, as a hypothesis, is quite unverifiable. You cannot refute it by pointing to an evil whose cause cannot be discovered and removed, any more than you can refute the more general hypothesis, of which this is little more than an application, that every event has a cause. But, though unverifiable, neither is meaningless, for both point the way to a method of procedure. It cannot be said that that method of procedure, as applied to evil, is a fruitless one, or that it has been tried and found wanting. Godwin has every right to retort, like the defenders of Christianity, that it has not been tried at all.

But, it may be objected, if Godwin merely means that human wickedness has discoverable social causes, he may be justified in denying that man is naturally evil, but not in saying that he is naturally good. For this would seem to mean that goodness has no such causes. And that does not seem to be Godwin's contention. His ideal state is, he insists, 'a state of high civilisation'. If goodness and wickedness are both the product of certain social conditions, why should one be called 'natural' any more than the other? The answer is that Godwin does mean something else as well by 'natural goodness'. He means, as we have seen, that the appropriate emotions will come of themselves when men see things as they are. We have yet to examine this contention; and it may turn out to be another unverifiable hypothesis, and possibly a misleading one. But at least this is not crass optimism of the kind with which Godwin is usually charged; for he never suggests that seeing things as they are is easy, or even finally attainable. Man is necessarily 'shut in on all sides': the causes of prejudice are innumerable and far-reaching, and can only be eliminated, if at all, by centuries of patient effort.

This brings us to the second charge in the usual indictment of Godwin: that he put too much trust in reason. To say that it is only necessary to show men things as they are is to say that man is a reasonable being (in the more optimistic sense of the phrase); and in fact he is not. And this is after all what is meant by the doctrine of original sin: man is moved by all sorts of lusts and passions, many of them evil; to get him to desire something it is not enough to demonstrate to him that it is desirable.

Now this charge badly needs clarifying. To say that man is not reasonable may mean many things. To distinguish two of them, which the critics of Godwin do not always distinguish, it may mean: (a) that, as Hume said, "'tis not contrary to reason to prefer the destruction of the whole world to the scratching of my finger'; i.e. man is not moved by reason in the sense that he cannot be, as a matter of logic; reason can lead us to conclusions about what is, but we cannot infer what ought to be from what is; or (b) that, while it is quite possible to demonstrate that a man ought to do so-and-so, that will not in practice be enough to make him do it; i.e. for man to be moved by reason is, not a logical, but a psychological impossibility. We have seen Godwin's answer to (a) and we may postpone further discussion of it till the next section; it is (b) that is relevant here.

To ask whether man is or is not a reasonable being in this sense is little more profitable than to ask whether he is 'naturally' good or 'naturally' evil. Men do sometimes, as we say, 'listen to reason'; very often they do not. But we had better see what Godwin really says about this, and whether what he says is patently absurd.

Godwin does of course say that to see that something is desirable is necessarily to desire it. Furthermore, he thinks

that there is, in the long run, no other way to make men do
what is desirable apart from making them see that it is desirable. That is why he resolutely sets his face against what
we have called the gospel of indirection in all its forms. This
is usually taken to mean that Godwin thought he could reform mankind by exposing it to a long series of syllogisms.
But his own account of the process is rather different.

Consider what he says about making the rich man renounce
his property. It is possible, Godwin suggests, for a rich man
to see that his riches do not really bring much happiness to
himself, and do cause great suffering to others; 'to have these
ideas so repeatedly suggested to his mind, so strongly impressed, and so perpetually haunting him, as finally to induce
a rich man to desire, with respect to personal gratifications,
to live as if he were a poor one'. It is possible; but it is
not, Godwin agrees, at all likely, and he is very far from
relying on such a change of heart. What he thinks is likely,
given the right social conditions, is that the poor and those
who are not personally affected one way or the other will
come to feel that great wealth is shameful. How will this affect
the rich man?

We have already seen, that the great incitement to the acquisition of wealth, is the love of distinction. Suppose then that, instead of the false glare which wealth, through the present puerility
of the human mind, reflects on his possessor, his conduct in
amassing and monopolising it, were seen in its true light. We
should not then demand his punishment, but we should look upon
him as a man uninitiated in the plainest sentiments of reason. He
would not be pointed at with the finger, or hooted as he passed
along through the resorts of men, but he would be conscious that
he was looked upon as the meanest of mankind. He would be
incited to the same assiduity in hiding his acquisitions then, as he
employs in displaying them now.[1]

[1] *P.J.* ii. 473.

Under these circumstances, it would no longer be surprising if the rich man came to renounce his riches. It will be seen that Godwin does not rely entirely on the power of reason. He is also calling into play the appetite for prestige, and the tendency of the normal man to conform to the prevailing sentiments in his community. There is certainly nothing wildly improbable in the situation he imagines. His rich man does violence to human nature no more than, let us say, the citizen of our own time who feels it his duty to sacrifice ease and comfort, and to risk his life, in time of war. Indeed, something like the change he describes is now taking place in the general attitude to noble birth, and is having its effect on the nobly born themselves. In the eighteenth century this would have seemed quite as unlikely.

But, it will be asked, what now becomes of Godwin's opposition to the gospel of indirection, or of his assertion that to think something desirable is to desire it? The rich man, it seems, is to be influenced after all by the indirect motive of prestige. And, on Godwin's own showing, the conviction that it is unjust to have great wealth will not, by itself, be enough to make him renounce his riches.

Godwin's reply would be, I think, to point out that he had never denied that the desire for prestige, and all the other passions that can be loosely lumped together under the name of self-interest, always will be powerful human motives. He does not want to eliminate them, but only to channel them in a different direction. What is important is that the direction they take shall be such that 'reflection confirms our choice'. In the example given, it will not be enough if the mass of the community come to despise the rich man out of mere envy, while secretly wishing to emulate him. It will then hardly be possible for him to share their sentiments: baulked in his desire for approval, he will merely become bitter and angry. The desire for prestige must be reinforced by the conviction that the community has right on its side. But the power of prejudice, and of self-deception, is so great that we are not likely to reach this conviction without the aid of such motives as the appetite for approval.

But does this answer the objection? Isn't it rather to concede the point, and admit that to think something desirable is not, after all, to desire it? To understand Godwin's position we need to keep in mind the distinction between rules of thumb and *scientia intuitiva*. To be convinced, in the full sense of the word, of the injustice of great inequality of wealth, it is necessary to understand in detail the suffering it causes. The member of a shipwrecked party who kept a secret store of food for himself and refused to share it with his starving companions might soon come to have such a conviction. To make him change his mind, no other motive might be necessary but the desire to relieve the suffering he saw in front of his eyes. But in a complex society we can hardly have this intimate and detailed knowledge. The belief in the injustice of inequality must always be, to a greater or lesser extent, a rule of thumb. We do not desire equality because we do not, in the full sense of *know*, know that it is desirable. We can always shut our eyes to the suffering of the poor, or persuade ourselves that there is no remedy for it. It is in this way that prejudice can conquer truth. But prejudice cannot continue to conquer if our eyes are open to all the facts. What the desire for approval does, in Godwin's example, is to force the rich man to open his eyes to them. He has to consider the sentiments of his fellow citizens. That is why it is important that the general disapproval of wealth shall be for the right reasons. Otherwise the rich man's eyes will be opened to quite a different set of facts: e.g. the enviousness of his countrymen. That is why Godwin opposes indirection, and that is what he means by saying that, in the last resort, we must trust to reason.

He may be right or he may be wrong; but at least it cannot fairly be said that he simply ignores 'the primal, brute forces in human nature that oppose reason'. What he does say is that these forces need not always oppose reason. They can be made to co-operate with it. Hartley had shown that motives like benevolence arise out of self-interest, by association. The desire for approval, for example, may be associated with the renunciation of wealth, not with its acquisition. It is not necessary, then, for man to become a passionless thinking machine: what is necessary is that he shall form the right associations. The right associations are those which he does form when he has access to all the facts. The great obstacle in the way is not so much human nature as the practical impossibility of having access to all the facts. Reason is powerful because it has the function of revealing facts. It is not opposed to passion as such, but only to those passions that depend on partial blindness or ignorance. Strictly speaking, reason cannot conquer passion: only passion can do that. But there are passions that arise when we know all the relevant facts, and passions that arise when we know only some of them. This is Spinoza's distinction between active and passive emotions. The two are not simply opposed, as 'good' and 'evil' forces in man's nature: the passive emotion is transformed into the corresponding active emotion. In something the same way, the lower pleasures, in Hartley's scheme, are taken up into the higher pleasures, which could not exist without them. Godwin is following Hartley in his treatment of the rich man's desire for prestige. He may not also have been directly influenced by Spinoza, but he comes very close to him. He would agree, for example, that we cannot continue to feel resentment towards someone who has injured us once we realize that our enemy is the helpless victim of circumstances. Our resentment does not simply vanish: it is directed against the whole human situation, and, as far as our enemy himself is concerned, is transformed into pity. But, whichever psychology Godwin is adopting, he is not simply ignoring the passions, or simply opposing reason to them. A statement like 'reason is not an independent principle, and has no tendency to excite us to action', even if he did add it in the third edition of *Political Justice*, is not, for Godwin, simply an afterthought.

2

One obstacle in the way of assessing Godwin fairly today is that he uses concepts and categories that we have discarded. His moral philosophy is put in terms of a faculty psychology which leads him to hypostatize 'Reason' and to ask whether men are motivated by 'Universal Benevolence'. We do not feel that we can either agree or disagree. Our first question is: what does this really mean? We cannot begin to discuss his philosophy until we have translated it into our own idiom.

I am going to begin, then, by summarizing what I take to be Godwin's basic beliefs. The danger in this procedure is that it gives us not so much Godwin as a twentieth-century gloss on Godwin. With this reservation I think we can say that Godwin's basic beliefs are three: one about ethics, one about logic, and one about social psychology. They are:

1. To be virtuous is to feel the right emotions. The right emotions are those that men do feel when they see all the facts clearly. When we analyse these emotions, we find that they are all consistent with the greatest happiness principle and the principle of impartiality.

2. True knowledge is of particulars, and all generalizations are, if not false, at least seriously misleading.

3. The generalizations men believe depend on the political institutions they live under.

Let us amplify these a little.

1. To be virtuous is to feel the appropriate emotions in a given situation. In the last analysis statements about morals are expressions of feeling. But this does not mean that we cannot reason about them. There are good or bad reasons for feeling frightened, or angry. Fear is appropriate in a given situation if the situation is one of danger. If we want to make someone feel the appropriate emotion (e.g. if we see a child about to pick up a poisonous snake) we do it by telling him facts that he does not know: we shout: 'Look out! That snake will bite!' If this doesn't impress him, we feel sure that it is because he doesn't understand about bites in general, and snake-bites in particular. We do not doubt that, if once we make him see the full facts of the situation, the emotion will come of its own accord. In the same way, if we want men to feel the appropriate emotions of benevolence, pity, affection, &c. to their fellows, we can do it by making them realize the full facts about human beings. It is in this sense that men are naturally good.

2. But, as we have just seen, it is possible to know, in a sense, that snakes bite, without feeling the appropriate emotion. A boy says, out of bravado: 'I don't care if it does bite me', and someone answers: 'Ah, you wouldn't say that if you'd seen your Uncle Henry die in agony.' The boy knows that snakes bite, as a generalization; he does not know the particulars which the generalization expresses. Which is to say that he does not really know the generalization at all.

But of course we cannot do without generalizations. It is impossible to know every particular in all its particularity. Here, then, is an inescapable source of error. It is particularly likely to mislead us in our judgements of human beings and of human actions: for every human being is unique. Since we cannot know every one intimately, we have to rely on generalizations, any one of which may be seriously misleading when applied to any given individual. Such generalizations form, as it were, a distorting glass through which we look at the world. And, since virtue depends on feeling the appropriate emotions toward other human beings, this is an adequate explanation of human frailty. This is what Godwin means by prejudice.

3. In practice the particular distorting glasses we use are, as it were, handed out to us by the governments under which we live. Our opinions about how human beings actually behave are influenced by concepts derived from legal institutions, like 'thief' or 'murderer', or concepts derived from social institutions, like 'lord' or 'pauper'. These stereotypes come between us and the actual human beings about us, so that we see, not them, but 'the growth and painting of our minds'. The institution of punishment has a special distorting effect, because it fosters the fiction of free will, and encourages emotions which are quite inappropriate to a creature who cannot really help any of his actions. Our opinions about how human beings ought to behave are distorted by concepts like 'honour' and 'virtue', which stem directly from political institutions, in the way Montesquieu had made clear. And that is what Godwin means by the corrupting effect of government.

The conclusions that follow from these three basic beliefs are:

1. If we want to improve human beings, we must help them to see things, and particularly each other, as they are.

2. This can be done: (*a*) by simplifying society, (*b*) by sweeping away social categories, like rank, and the legal categories that depend on punishment, (*c*) by encouraging individual judgement, so that men will no longer trust to rules of thumb.

Now let us see what can be said about these beliefs.

1. I have condensed Godwin's ethics to three propositions; and each of these is, to say the least, highly doubtful.

We have already seen that Godwin is in doubt whether to say that virtue consists in feeling the right emotions or in seeing which emotions are the right ones. Is virtue, that is to say, 'the desire to promote the happiness of all intelligent beings' or the conviction that the happiness of all intelligent beings is desirable? It is because Godwin does not make this distinction that he is able to say that men's voluntary actions originate in their opinions (i.e. their opinions about what is desirable); whereas all he is entitled to say is that they originate in their desires. To say 'X is good' no doubt is to say 'X is desirable'; but that is not to say 'X is desired'. And this remains true even if it is conceded that the conviction that X is desirable is itself an emotion: which is all that Hutcheson maintained.

Now this strikes at the heart of Godwin's system. For, if it is possible to be convinced that X is desirable without desiring X, it follows that more may be needed to reform men's conduct than an appeal to reason. And this is of course what Godwin's critics have always said.

Godwin's reply is that no one is fully convinced that X is desirable unless he is fully seized of the facts on which that conclusion is based. This is the way that the spectator, in Hume's illustration, becomes convinced that the rescue of the shipwrecked sailors is desirable. To grasp all that is involved in their suffering is both to think that their rescue is desirable and to desire it. The two are hardly separable. The only reason we commonly suppose that it is possible to think X desirable without desiring X is that by 'thinking X desirable' we usually mean something less than a full conviction, based on an intimate knowledge of all the facts: we mean a rule of thumb.

Godwin, in short, escapes from the objections we have

raised to the first of these three propositions by falling back on the second. To be virtuous is to feel the emotions that men do feel when they know all the facts. But even if we grant that thinking (or feeling) X desirable is not, under these circumstances, really different from desiring X, there is still a clear distinction between our knowledge of the facts and the emotions that arise from that knowledge. Because the knowledge is true knowledge it does not follow that the emotions are 'right'. To suppose that they are is a pure hypothesis. It may be a reasonable hypothesis; but it needs to be verified.

The truth is, however, that it cannot be verified. For if anyone produces an instance of a man who is fully seized of all the relevant facts and still does not feel the right emotions, the reply will simply be: 'But in that case he cannot really understand all the relevant facts.' If the ship in our illustration is sunk by an enemy aeroplane, and the pilot watches all the scenes that Hume describes with callous delight, Godwin will certainly say: 'Ah, but he is blinded by prejudice; he does not really understand what he sees.' Now there are good reasons for saying this: we know, as a matter of experience, that people who do behave in this way in war-time view the same scenes quite differently in times of peace. Nevertheless, it may be said that there is no sure way of knowing whether anyone 'knows the full facts' or not. Feeling 'the right emotions' is taken as proof of knowing them; and, conversely, not feeling them is taken as proof of prejudice.

Much the same may be said of our third proposition, about the greatest happiness principle. I do not think that Godwin seriously attempts to prove this: he simply assumes it. Later the opponents of utilitarianism attempted to disprove it by finding negative instances: actions which we agree to call right, but which do not make for the greatest happiness of the greatest number. The favourite ones are promise-keeping, and family obligations. The utilitarian usually denies that these are negative instances; and he can make out a fair case. But if this defence fails, it is always open to him to say that these actions are not right after all, and that we are mistaken in supposing that they are. Godwin does actually take this line both about family obligations ('the famous fire cause') and about promise-keeping. And this means of course that the greatest happiness principle can never be disproved.

It is, then, not unfair to say that the whole of Godwin's moral philosophy is a mere tissue of assumptions. His basic hypotheses are not merely unverified, but intrinsically unverifiable. What he is really saying is that, if we could see things as they are, we would not only feel convinced that universal benevolence is desirable, but would also all feel benevolent to all men. This is the dogma of natural goodness. Since he also admits that it is ultimately impossible to see things as they are, this hypothesis must remain untested. Those who say that it has been disproved by the facts are quite wrong. The truth is that it could not be disproved by any facts. But that may well be a much more damning criticism.

At the same time, there is something to be said in Godwin's defence. Modern writers on ethics have been puzzled to explain in what sense ethical propositions can be supported by reasons. It is indeed demonstrable that they cannot be. You cannot argue from what is to what ought to be unless you already assume something about what ought to be. At least these basic assumptions, then, cannot be supported by any reasons. Nevertheless, we do find ourselves adducing facts in support of our moral convictions, and we do find that we can sometimes change the convictions of our friends by advancing these reasons.

The conclusion is sometimes drawn that the connexion between *X is* and *Y ought to be* is not a logical but a psychological one. That is to say, it is a fact that you can make human beings think *Y ought to be* by convincing them that *X is*; but the truth of *X is* does not guarantee the truth of *Y ought to be*. Either ethical propositions are not capable of being true or false, or, if they are, we can never have good reasons for supposing that they are.

Now one way of avoiding these conclusions is to take it for granted that *Y ought to be* is true if we do find ourselves believing it when we believe that *X is*, and if *X is* is true.

But this may take us further than we want to go. For sometimes we want to say that men are wrong in the moral inferences they draw. For example, Godwin thought that men were wrong in supposing that, if anyone has committed a crime, then he ought to be punished. But he would hardly deny that men do think in this way. We want, in short, to say that the reasons brought in support of moral propositions may be good or bad reasons. What is the criterion of a bad reason? I think Godwin would say that the proof that 'If *A* has committed a crime, he ought to be punished' is false is that we do not continue to hold it if we know further facts about the committing of crimes, the facts which the determinist alleges, and which Godwin accepted. A bad reason, then, is one that does not continue to be effective when we know all the facts; and a good one is one that does.

Now this means that we must assume two things. We must assume that, if men knew all the facts, they would draw the same moral conclusions from them. If, as Godwin believed, to know all is to pardon all, then *A*'s not pardoning all is proof that he does not know all. We must dismiss the possibility that *A* can know all and pardon all and *B* know all and not pardon all. Secondly, if it is true that to know all is to pardon all, we must assume that it is right to pardon all. We must not say that this merely proves that human beings are at bottom sentimental.

These two assumptions are the doctrines that human beings are reasonable and that they are 'naturally good'. There are grave difficulties in the way of accepting either of them. But at least it can be said that, if we do accept them, we can go on supposing that there are good reasons for believing moral propositions. At any rate this seems to be as tenable as any of the alternative explanations of how this is possible.

2. True knowledge is of particulars, and generalizations are, if not false, at least misleading.

Godwin was not a logician or an epistemologist, and it is perhaps misleading to put the second of his basic beliefs in this form. He applies it chiefly to human beings; and it might be fairer to say simply that he believed in the uniqueness of every human being, and every human action. That is the basis of his objection to law. No one action is quite like another: no two murders, for example, are committed from quite the same motives; human motives, indeed, are almost infinitely complex.

Lawyers have not the faculty of unlimited prescience, and cannot define that which is boundless. The alternative that remains is, either to wrest the law to include a case which was never in the contemplation of its authors, or to make a new law to provide for this particular case. Much has been done in the first of these modes. The quibbles of lawyers, and the arts by which they refine and distort the sense of the law, are proverbial. But, though much is done, everything cannot be thus done. . . . It is therefore perpetually necessary to make new laws. . . . The volume in which justice records her prescriptions is for ever increasing, and the world would not contain the books that might be written.[1]

And the result, he suggests, is that the law loses its one advantage, certainty. 'Laws were made, to put an end to ambiguity, and that each man might know what he had to expect. . . . Law was made, that a plain man might know what

[1] *P.J.* ii. 400.

he had to expect; and yet the most skilful practitioners differ about the event of my suit.'[1] And there is an even more serious consequence. 'Law tends, no less than creeds, catechisms and tests, to fix the human mind in a stagnant condition.'[2]

Now whatever may be thought about this criticism of law, there is a good deal to be said in support of the principle that human beings are unique. It is certainly easier to defend than the generalization about generalizations. And, it may be asked, if this was what Godwin chiefly meant, why saddle him with the much more vulnerable opinion?

The answer is that for Godwin there is a general problem of error. 'Man, considered in himself, is merely a being capable of impression, a recipient of sensations.'[3] But how, then, does he come to make mistakes? The camera cannot lie. Godwin does not raise this question specifically, but I think his answer is implicit in what he says about abstraction. 'Abstraction indeed . . . is in some sort coeval with and inseparable from the existence of mind. The next step to simple perception is that of comparison. . . . Comparison immediately leads to imperfect abstraction. The sensation of to-day is classed, if similar, with the sensation of yesterday, and an inference is made respecting the conduct to be adopted.' In a footnote, he adds that 'the human mind is perhaps incapable of entertaining any but general ideas. Take, for example, a wine-glass. If, after this glass is withdrawn, I present to you another from the same set, you will probably be unable to determine whether it is another or the same. . . . It is impossible so to individualize our remarks as to cause our idea to be truly particular, and not special.' And, significantly, he concludes from this that there are no 'perfect ideas', but only imperfect ones, which may be of three kinds: 'imperfect, such as those which are produced in us, by a near and careful inspection of any visible object; imperfect, such as those pro-

[1] *P.J.* ii. 401.   [2] Ibid. 403.   [3] Ibid. 78.

duced by a slight and distant view; imperfect, so as to have no resemblance to an image of any external object. The perception produced in us in slight and current discourse by the words, river, field, are of this nature; and have no more resemblance to the image of any visible object than the perception ordinarily produced in us by the words, conquest, government, virtue.'[1]

Generalization, then, is at once the source of knowledge and of error. Without it we could not organize our perceptions; but without it, we could not commit the follies that we do commit. As he puts it in *Thoughts on Man*: 'It is thus that we arrive at science, and go forward to those subtleties, and that perspicuity of explanation, which place man in a distinct order of being, leaving all the other inhabitants of earth at an immeasurable distance below him . . . But in certain respects we pay a very high price for this distinction. It is to it that we must impute all the follies, extravagances and hallucinations of human intellect.'[2] And the way to avoid these extravagances is to test our generalizations by applying them whenever possible to concrete instances.

It would take us too far afield to criticize this position in detail; and in any case we would be treading well-worn ground. But it may be noticed that this position is not quite consistent with what Godwin says about the power of reason. The classic rationalist position is that reason enables us to penetrate beyond the deceitful appearances of things, as revealed in sensation, to their hidden essences. It is because reason deals with this underlying reality that it cannot lead us astray. It is hard to maintain this conclusion if you say that reason deals with general ideas which are necessarily imperfect approximations to the particulars which are alone real.

The difficulty comes out in Godwin's treatment of free will. So far as we have direct acquaintance with the working of our

[1] Ibid. i. 113–14.   [2] *Thoughts on Man* (London, 1831), p. 244.

own minds, he says, we feel, quite irresistibly, 'a delusive
sense of liberty'. 'Thus . . . we have demonstration, all the
powers of our reasoning faculty, on one side, and the feeling
of our minds, an inward persuasion of which with all our
efforts we can never divest ourselves, on the other.'[1] Significantly, he compares this sense of liberty with our conviction
that secondary qualities are really in external objects. 'It
never occurs to us, when occupied with the affairs of actual
life, that there is no heat in fire, and no colour in the rainbow.'[2]
This looks as if the senses are not, after all, the last court of
appeal.

The point is important, because Godwin's determinism is
in many ways central to his whole philosophy. The right
emotions are those that we feel when we see human beings as
they really are; and one of the biggest obstacles in the way of
feeling them is the delusive sense of liberty and the concepts
of guilt, sin, and the rest to which it gives rise.

I regard you as vicious [says Mr. Collins to Caleb Williams],
but I do not consider the vicious as proper objects of indignation.
I consider you as a machine; you are not constituted, I am afraid,
to be greatly useful to your fellow men: but you did not make yourself; you are just what circumstances irresistibly impelled you to
be. I am sorry for your ill properties; but I entertain no enmity
against you, nothing but benevolence.[3]

And in *Thoughts on Man* Godwin tells us that the great
value of determinism is that, if we hold it:

We shall learn, according to the apostolic precept, to 'be angry,
and sin not, neither let the sun go down upon our wrath'. We shall
make of our fellow-men neither idols to worship, nor demons to be
regarded with horror and execration. . . . And, most of all, we shall
view with pity, even with sympathy, the men whose frailties we
behold, or by whom crimes are perpetrated, satisfied that they are

---

[1] *Thoughts on Man*, p. 230.   [2] Ibid., p. 241.
[3] *Caleb Williams* (Routledge, 1903), p. 430.

parts of one great machine, and, like ourselves, are driven forward by impulses over which they have no real control.[1]

But, if this is the right attitude to humanity, it is not so certain that it will come automatically if we live in small communities and are intimately acquainted with our neighbours. On Godwin's own showing, this is a truth that comes only to 'the philosopher in his closet'. No doubt we do need to see in detail how it applies to particular individuals, before it can move us in practice; but mere acquaintance with individuals is not enough. In this crucial matter, the complexity of generalizations is not the sole source of error.

There is a further objection. Godwin assumes that man is a machine for the recording of impressions, and that the only source of error is the attempt to take in more than can be assimilated. But in his essay *Of Belief* he admits that there may be internal sources of error.

In every question of paramount importance there is ever a secret influence urging me earnestly to desire to find one side of the question right and the other wrong. Shall I be a Whig or a Tory, believe a republic or a mixed monarchy most conducive to the improvement and happiness of mankind, embrace the creed of free will or necessity? There is in all cases a 'strong temptation that waketh in the heart'. Cowardice urges me to become the adherent of that creed, which is espoused by my nearest friends, or those who are most qualified to serve me. Enterprise and a courageous spirit on the contrary bid me embrace the tenet, the embracing of which shall most conduce to my reputation for extraordinary perspicuity and acuteness, and gain me the character of an intrepid adventurer, a man who dares commit himself to an unknown voyage.[2]

There are, in fact, two kinds of prejudice: a preconceived opinion on some matter of fact, and a desire to believe something for reasons which have nothing to do with its truth or

[1] *Thoughts on Man*, p. 242.   [2] Ibid., pp. 247–8.

falsity. The first may no doubt be corrected by a closer acquaintance with the facts; but how shall we root out the second?

I think that Godwin made light of this difficulty because he was influenced by the arguments of the egoists. If to think something desirable is to believe that it gives me pleasure, then my secret desires are not finally at variance with my beliefs about public questions. I want to be thought a bold thinker because that will give me pleasure; to ask whether I should be a Whig or a Tory is to ask which will give me most pleasure. More generally, if we ought to follow the evidence wherever it leads, this is because we will gain most pleasure from doing so. In the long run, then, the desires that make me rationalize will also make me seek the truth; there is no final cleavage between the two. If I knew all the facts I would know that adopting a true opinion would give me more pleasure in the long run than shocking the Philistines; so that my desire for notoriety would be driven out by my desire to know the truth.

The case is altered if to think something desirable is to think it 'conducive to the happiness of mankind'. There is now a real cleavage between my secret desires and my desire to know the truth, and something more than a full knowledge of all the facts may be needed to vanquish those desires. The obvious next step is to suppose that all desires can be reduced to the one desire for human happiness (universal benevolence) just as the egoist had said that they could be reduced to self-interest. As we have seen, this is a step that Godwin does not quite take, though he goes a long way towards taking it.

Instead, he is inclined to fall back on Hartley's argument that all our desires are generated from self-interest by association. But this does not mean that there can be no conflict between them. It is here that the latent contradiction between Godwin's rationalism and his sensationalism shows itself.

If we come to desire the general happiness because of associations with our own happiness, and the two are not necessarily connected, then our desire is fundamentally irrational. Indeed this kind of association would seem to be what is meant by prejudice, and it would seem to be the function of reason to destroy such associations. If, instead, 'reflection confirms our choice', this can only mean that we see that the general happiness is desirable quite apart from our own happiness. But apparently we could not desire human happiness unless we had once erroneously associated it with our own happiness. This looks as if Burke is right after all, and prejudice is a necessary part of human virtue.

At bottom, then, Godwin has two inconsistent beliefs about generalizations which he never really reconciles. One is that generalization is the sole cause of error, and that we must see things as they are if life is made so simple that we can readily test every generalization by the particulars which constitute its meaning. The other is that we are led into error by our initial bias in favour of our own pleasure, and that we cannot see things as they are until we grasp the principle of impartiality. But this is attained by reason, which means by abstraction and generalization; so that it seems that there is in 'human nature' a source of error that can only be corrected by generalization.

3. The generalizations men believe depend on the political institutions they live under.

I have interpreted this as an anticipation of the modern anthropologist's belief in the all-pervading influence of 'the culture pattern'. That belief is still a subject of controversy, and it is fortunately not necessary for me to try to decide the controversy here.

Something must, however, be said about Godwin's application of the theory and the conclusions he draws from it. For there are two important differences between Godwin and the modern anthropologists. He says that 'government' is the cause of our beliefs: they say 'the culture', or society. Further, he thinks of these beliefs as distorting glasses, which we can and should discard; without government we will see things as they are. They would say that 'culture' can never be discarded.

The two differences are connected. For Godwin wants to discard government, but not society. He is inclined to say that the choice is between seeing the facts in all their naked individuality, and seeing them through the distorting medium of political ideologies. But, just as 'the human mind is incapable of entertaining any but general ideas', so it is impossible to look at the facts except in the light of some ideology. Godwin's ideal society engenders a very definite set of beliefs: in equality, in the iniquity of property, in the injustice of punishment, and so on. These beliefs colour our judgement of men's actions and characters just as the beliefs in honour or in virtue colour them. But the beliefs of his ideal society, Godwin would say, are true. The opposition is not really between beliefs engendered by social institutions, which are necessarily false, and the beliefs that arise without social institutions, which are necessarily true; it is between true beliefs and false beliefs, each of which may be engendered by social institutions. And this means that we cannot simply assume that the beliefs that arise in the anarchic society are true: we must prove this independently.

This criticism is, in one way, not very damaging to Godwin. For he is not really a primitivist; and of course he does not deny that it is possible to arrive at true beliefs in spite of the effect of social prejudice. It is indeed an essential part of his position that men are bound to glimpse at least some part of the truth in spite of prejudice. But this means, of course, that men's beliefs do not depend entirely on the political institutions they live under. In this he differs from at least some modern anthropologists, who are inclined to say that value judgements (in Godwin's language, 'opinions about what is desirable') are entirely 'a function of the culture', and that the question is not whether they are true or false, but whether they are appropriate to a given society; so that it is impossible to judge between the beliefs of two different societies. There are grave objections to this position, and it is hardly a fault in Godwin that he did not hold it.

It may be argued, however, that he ought to have held it; for it does follow from some of his basic assumptions. If opinions about what is desirable arise, as Hartley had suggested, from associations with self-interest, and if the associations we form depend on the society we live in, then this conclusion is unavoidable. Godwin could only avoid it by asserting that it is possible for reason either to confirm or reject our opinion; and, as we have seen, it is not clear how he reconciles this assertion with his associationism.

The point may be put in terms of Godwin's determinism. Men are not to be blamed for their actions, because their actions are determined by their opinions, and their opinions are themselves determined. Determined by what? Partly, it seems, by the associations they happen to have formed, and partly by reason; and there is a conflict between these two. But what determines the issue of the conflict? Temperament, upbringing, the social and intellectual climate? But, if it is any of these, then this is what determines our opinions. For to talk of truth vanquishing prejudice is merely to say that a true opinion replaces a false one, and to say that an opinion has conquered is to say that we believe it to be true. If the case is put in the way Godwin puts it, there seems no escape from the conclusion that our opinion about what is true is determined by some quite irrelevant factor. Godwin wants 'truth' to come in at some indefinite point as a quite undetermined factor, in the way that the anti-determinists want 'free will' to come in; and he is faced with exactly the same difficulty as they.

Godwin's determinism is of a rather unusual kind. When he talks about freeing Hartley's system from 'the scheme of material automatism with which it was unnecessarily clogged', he means, among other things, to question the assumption that physical causes are the basic ones. Mental phenomena are, he thinks, governed by causal laws no less than physical phenomena, but this does not mean that they are ultimately reducible to physical phenomena. Hobbes had thought that thinking could ultimately be explained in terms of motion; and it is this tradition that made Hartley try to explain the mechanism of association in terms of 'vibratiuncles'. The tradition is continued by those modern psychologists who define an 'attitude of mind' as the reflection in consciousness of a 'motor set' of the body.

Godwin, on the other hand, is much closer to Berkeley, who took willing as the basic type of causal process. Berkeley and the materialists were, of course, alike in thinking that, since matter and mind interact, one of them must ultimately be reducible to the other. The only question was: which? Godwin differs from both parties in taking up a dualist position. In the later editions of *Political Justice*, he seizes on Hume's analysis of causation as justifying this dualism. To say that mind affects matter, or that matter affects mind, is merely to say that, as a fact of experience, mental events and physical events are found in conjunction; and there is no difficulty about saying this.

It is of no importance that we cannot see the ground of that necessity, or imagine how sensations, pleasurable or painful, when presented to the mind of a percipient being, are able to generate volition and animal motion; for, if there be any truth in the above statement, we are equally incapable of perceiving a ground of connection between any two events in the material universe, the

common and received opinion, that we do perceive such ground
of connection, being in reality, nothing more than a vulgar prejudice.[1]

In saying that volitions are determined, then, Godwin
does not want to explain away volition. Mental events have
their place in the chain of cause and effect: physical events
have mental causes just as mental events have physical
causes. Godwin often talks quite rhapsodically about 'the
power of mind'. The most notorious instance is the chapter
in *Political Justice* in which he suggests, quite in the spirit of
Shaw's *Back to Methusaleh*, that perhaps the men of the
future will learn to live for hundreds of years and outgrow
their childish preoccupation with physical pleasure.[2] For
Godwin accepts Hume's thesis with a difference. He does
not deny that there is a necessary connexion between cause
and effect but only that we can ever understand its nature. 'We
cannot', he says, 'discover the causes of things, or ascertain
that in the antecedent which connects it with the consequent,
and discern nothing but their contiguity.'[3] In saying, then,
that volitions figure in the chain of cause and effect, Godwin
is saying that 'desire' (and, more generally, 'Mind') is a real
force in the world. There are times indeed when, reading
Godwin, one feels uneasily that he may at any moment begin
to talk of Thinking the Right Thoughts and Tapping the
Hidden Power Within.

But volitions, though of real importance, are themselves
determined. They are not, however, always determined by
physical causes. It is true that, in the passage quoted above,
he speaks of 'pleasurable and painful sensations' as the common causes of volition; and this is very like what Hobbes had
said. But a little later he adds this:

The character of any man is the result of a long series of impressions, communicated to his mind and modifying it in a certain

[1] *P.J.* i. 368–9.   [2] Ibid. ii. 519–29.   [3] Ibid. i. 94.

manner, so as to enable us, a number of these modifications and
impressions being given, to predict his conduct. Hence arise his
temper and habits, respecting which we reasonably conclude, that
they will not be abruptly superseded and reversed; and that, if
ever they be reversed, it will not be accidentally, but in consequence of some strong reason persuading, or some extraordinary
event modifying his mind.[1]

The distinction between 'a strong reason persuading' and
'some extraordinary event modifying' is important. Men are
subject to persuasion as well as to conditioning. Anything
counts as the cause of an opinion that constantly precedes it;
and we find that these antecedents are of very different
kinds. No doubt it is true that a man with influenza cannot
help taking a gloomy view of life; but it is also true that a man
who has grasped the premisses of a syllogism cannot help
assenting to the conclusion. Either of these is, for Godwin,
a determining factor; and he tends to think of life as a battle
between these two kinds of determinant, much as his Puritan
forebears thought of it as a struggle between good and evil.
The rallying-cry is: Truth versus Prejudice!

The battle is not for the soul of man: it is for his opinions
about what things are desirable. If we discount the strong
moralizing strain in Godwin, we have here a further resemblance to the modern anthropologist. Godwin's 'opinions'
are very like their 'attitudes'.

Motive [say Godwin] may be distinguished, according to its
different relations, into direct and indirect; understanding by the
direct, that which is present to the mind of the agent at the time of
his determination, and which belongs to every voluntary action,
and to so much of every action as is voluntary; and by the indirect, that which operates without being adverted to by the mind,
whether in the case of actions originally involuntary, or that have
become so, in whole or in part, by the force of habit.[2]

[1] *P.J.* i. 370.   [2] Ibid. 431.

An opinion, that is to say, is complex, and some of its components are unconscious. Or, putting it another way, the determinants of opinion are manifold: ultimately they may even comprise the whole life-history of the man who holds the opinion. And this is very like the anthropologist's conception of attitudes emerging from the complicated network that he calls a culture-pattern. He too wants to say that attitudes have both physical and mental causes.

Does this enable Godwin to say that, among the determinants of opinion, there is something that can be called 'truth', or 'facts', or 'what is the case'? It seems sensible to say that, while education, or background, or peculiarities of temperament may lead us into false beliefs, we have also a capacity for seeing facts that enables us to correct these beliefs. Nevertheless, we can hardly talk about 'truth' as one determinant of opinion among others; we must rather say that, of the determinants of opinion, some lead us to form false beliefs and others to form true beliefs. It might be thought that, if Godwin cares to dramatize this as 'the struggle between truth and prejudice', no great harm has been done. But a difficulty still remains. We seem to be assuming that there are tests for truth which are quite distinct from the determinants of opinion; whereas what determines an opinion does so by determining what tests of truth we will accept.

The difficulty faces all who have entertained theories about what is currently called 'the sociology of knowledge', or 'cultural determinism'. If all opinions are socially determined, this applies to theories about the sociology of knowledge. And this means that we cannot say of such theories; 'this is true', but only 'this is what my social background determines me to believe'. Obviously the sociologist of knowledge wants to say more than this: he wants to break out of the charmed circle altogether. One way of avoiding this difficulty is to say that our theories apply only to certain kinds of opinion: for example, value judgements or 'opinions about what is desirable'. And this involves us in saying that such judgements can never be known to be true or false, and are perhaps not capable of being true or false. Modern sociologists are inclined to say this, though not perhaps quite consistently.[1] But Godwin is emphatically not prepared to say this; he is quite sure that some things really are desirable, and can be known to be desirable.

I think this problem is a real one, and I do not pretend to know the answer. But it looks as if we cannot consistently regard our capacity for reasoning as one determinant of opinion of the same type as our social background or the inhibitions we acquired in infancy. The point may perhaps be put by saying that Godwin does not sufficiently distinguish between causal necessity and entailment or 'logical necessity.' But this is rather glib; for, while it is true that the conclusion of a syllogism follows from the premisses in quite a different sense from that in which a knee-jerk follows from the doctor's tap, it seems reasonable to say that, just as I cannot help jerking my knee, once I have been tapped, so I cannot help assenting to the conclusion once I have grasped the premisses. That is the point that Godwin insists on; but insisting on it does seem to raise some very difficult problems.

The point is, as I have already suggested, connected with Godwin's vacillation between Hartley's account of the nature of moral judgements, and Price's. He wants to say both that association (as opposed to reason) is a powerful source of prejudice, and that it is the psychological mechanism that makes moral judgements possible at all. And it is at least doubtful whether he can say both these things.

[1] The difficulty is that they usually interpret this statement itself as a value judgement, viz.: no value judgement is *to be preferred* to any other

INDEX

'Abstract', 57–61.
Adams, J., 70, 72, 109–10; quoted, 72–73, 110.
Affection: Godwin not opposing, 31–33; and *St. Leon*, 98, 119; change of opinion on, 118–20; as cause of prejudice, 143–5, 162–6.
Ambition, 95, 103–4.
Anti-Jacobin, 1, 3.
Arnold, T. W., 130.
Assemblies, national, 123–31.
Associations: Hartley on, 23–27; as cause of prejudice, 137–42, 153–5; Godwin inconsistent about, 195.

Benevolence, 40–48.
Bentham, J., 14, 15, 27, 102.
Berkeley, G., 106, 198.
Bonar, J., quoted, 82.
Brailsford, H. N., 6, 69.
Brown, Ford K., 100.
Burke, E., 59–60, 79, 141, 195; quoted, 4, 59, 60.
Butler, J., 40–48, 106.

Caleb Williams: and Godwin's social theory, 86–90, 94–97; and misunderstanding, 67; Stephen on, 68; title of, 28; mentioned, 3; quoted, 15, 86, 89, 90, 95, 97, 192.
Catholicism, Roman, 138–41.
Change, violent, 169–70.
Chatham, Life of, 2.
Chaucer, Life of, see *Life of Chaucer*.
Clarke, S., 36.
Cloudesley, 149–50.
Co-operation, 156.
Crotchet Castle, 157.
Culture pattern, 69, 78–85, 195–7.

Deloraine, 162.
Democracy, 123–31.
de Quincey, T., quoted, 4.
Despotism, 71, 90, 114.
Determinism: Godwin's version of, 29, 198–200; and punishment, 146; difficulties in, 191–3, 197–202.
Diary, Godwin's, quoted, 36, 39, 42, 69.
Domestic affection, *see* Affection.
Dubois, E., quoted, 57.
Duty, 19, 30.

Émile, 131, 155.
Enquirer, quoted, 103, 111, 112, 126.

First Principles of Morals, 37.
Fleetwood: and misunderstanding, 67, 144; and romanticism, 134–6; and Rousseau, 160; and associations, 153–4; quoted, 68, 119, 134, 135, 136, 171.
Fleisher, D., 6, 163; quoted, 172.
Frankness, 12, 101–2, 143, 162.

General will, 124–7.
Generalizations: and reason, 11; and knowledge, 53–54, 191; and prejudice, 32–35, 66, 143, 182, 183, 189–91; and associations, 137–40; Godwin inconsistent about, 193–5.
Gerrald, J., 86.
Goodness, Natural, 51–52, 175–6, 189.
Gray, A., 67.
Green, T., 15.

Happiness, Scale of, 90–94.
Hartley, D.: and associations, 17,

PRINTED IN
GREAT BRITAIN
AT THE
UNIVERSITY PRESS
OXFORD
BY
CHARLES BATEY
PRINTER
TO THE
UNIVERSITY